A CREATIVE DREAM IS:

SOMETHING THAT PULLS YOU, DRAWS YOU IN, CAUSES GLEE

SOMETHING YOU THINK ABOUT WITH GREAT relish, EAGERNESS, QUIET SATISFACTION or DELIGHT

SOMETHING YOU WOULD DO FOR FREE

SOMETHING YOU FEEL inspired TO SHARE

SOMETHING THAT occupies YOUR ATTENTION even WHILE DOING OTHER WORK

SOMETHING WITH it's own energy or MOMENTUM

SOMETHING exciting TO HEAR ABOUT or DO

SOMETHING FREE and AVAILABLE FOR everyone TO experience

SOMETHING unrelated PHYSICAL ABILITY

BEING CREATIVE and

Fireside

OTHER BOOKS BY SARK

WWW.PLANETSARK.COM

Make Your Creative Dreams Real

A plan for procrastinators, perfectionists, busy people, and people who would really rather sleep all day

SARK

A Fireside Book
Published by Simon & Schuster
New York · London · Toronto · Sydney

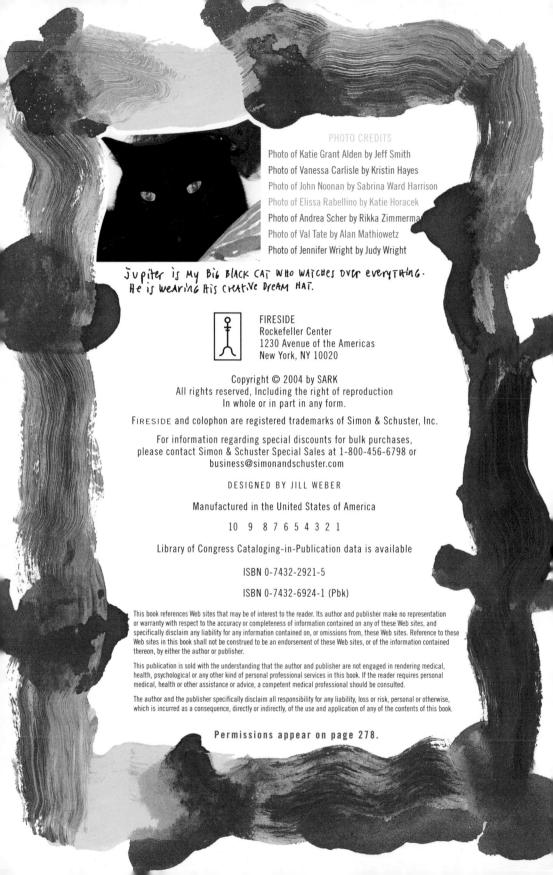

PHOTO CREDITS

Photo of Katie Grant Alden by Jeff Smith

Photo of Vanessa Carlisle by Kristin Hayes

Photo of John Noonan by Sabrina Ward Harrison

Photo of Elissa Rabellino by Katie Horacek

Photo of Andrea Scher by Rikka Zimmerma

Photo of Val Tate by Alan Mathiowetz

Photo of Jennifer Wright by Judy Wright

JUpiter is my BiG BLACK CAT WHo WATCHES OVEr everyTHiNG.
HE is weariNG His creaTiVE DreAM HAT.

FIRESIDE
Rockefeller Center
1230 Avenue of the Americas
New York, NY 10020

FIRESIDE and colophon are registered trademarks of Simon & Schuster, Inc.

For information regarding special discounts for bulk purchases,
please contact Simon & Schuster Special Sales at 1-800-456-6798 or
business@simonandschuster.com

DESIGNED BY JILL WEBER

Manufactured in the United States of America

10   9   8 7 6 5 4 3 2 1

Library of Congress Cataloging-in-Publication data is available

ISBN 0-7432-2921-5

ISBN 0-7432-6924-1 (Pbk)

Permissions appear on page 278.

THis BOOK is
DeDiCATeD TO
THe GRACe anD BeAUTY
of MY GODCHiLDReN
anD THeiR CReATiVe DReAMS
eMiLY · ZOe · VaNeSSA

MAY All of OUR CReaTiVe DReAMS HeAL AND
illUMiNATe THiS DeAR WORLD of OURS

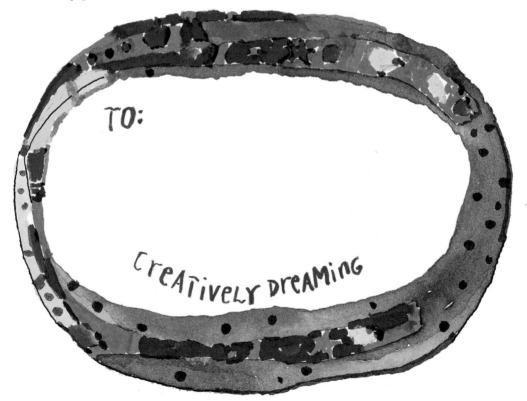

TO:

CReATiVeLY DReAMiNG

THIS is A non-linear TABLE of contents CALLED DREAMDOTS

if YOU ARE DELIGHTED BY order and DETAIL, GO TO PAGE 15 FOR A SECOND TABLE of contents

THIS is ABBREVIATED in content, just enough To Give YOU A TASTE...

FULL and COMPLETE TABLE of CONTENTS on PAGE: 15

AT THE end of
eACH CHAPTER Are
GAMES, GifTS,
CHALLenGeS and
resources

Introduction

I believe that creative dreams saved my life. As a young girl, I was physically and sexually abused by a family member, and my creative dreams were my haven and retreat from those experiences.

My creative dreams fueled me, filled me with wonder, and infused me with certainty that there was something in the world that was good.

I saw one of my first creative dreams come alive in the second grade when I came home from school and announced to my mother:

"I think that show-and-tell should be ME every day."

She explained that the other kids needed a chance too. I told her that the other kids wanted me to show and tell every day. I told them about the many things that

i used to fill small books with things I saw on the way to school...

happened to me on my walk to school. I saw and heard so many things that I wanted to share:

The gooseberry bush you could climb inside and then eat your way out of.

Ducks' feet on flat wet rocks in the creek.

The snapping turtle that lived under a large mossy log.

The woman with the big broom and the even bigger cat.

i WONDERED WHAT THE little Boy SAW

The angry German shepherd in the wire cage at the end of the alley.

The gang of kids down the block who rode in loud, fast cars.

The quiet boy who sat on his front step.

LUCKILY, my teacher saw my enthusiasm and sent me to other grades to do my show-and-tell. My teacher's support encouraged me to pay attention to such things and to develop my vision—skills I still use in writing my books. I am still paying close attention to my world and sharing it with others.

WHEN I WAS 10, my best friend was 80 years old. His name was Mr. Boggs. His house was my refuge. He and I discussed my creative dreams and he inspired me to tell stories about what I saw in the world.

Mr. Boggs became very ill and went into the hospital. My mother explained that because of his age and health, he probably wouldn't be coming home. I vowed to create something for him every day that he was in the hospital, and sent him handmade books, cards, and posters.

He did get out of the hospital, and when he did he said to me, "I think you saved my life. No one else called or wrote, and I had to get out to see you."

I immediately started writing my first book, because I thought that if my art and words could affect one person that much, what might happen if I could share them with the world?

A big creative dream was born that summer and it continues to live to this day.

FROM AGES 14 TO 26, I put my creative dreams on hold as I attended school and experimented with hundreds of part-time jobs.

When I was 26, I decided to make my creative dream of living as an artist and writer real. I began by creating art and writing to share with the world. For years, my art and writing was rejected by magazines, newspapers, and publishing companies. Although it must be said that I didn't send it out very often, because I was too busy surviving and crafting new work.

creative
Dreams
Grow
and
Bloom
even when
we're Not
WATCHing

dear
Mr.
Boggs

SO I WAS LIVING MY CREATIVE DREAM, but it wasn't yet making me a living. Then I had an important realization: since creative dreams had literally saved my life, perhaps it was time that I really gave life to my creative dreams.

Then, in 1988, I began to put all of myself into my work, with no thought of how it might look or seem to others, or whether it would be rejected.

I asked myself two questions:

What did I have to offer?
How could I be of use?

THE ANSWERS TO THOSE QUESTIONS came very quickly, in dreams.

I had my creative soul and dreams to offer, and I could be of use by letting my soul and creative dreams become visible and active.

My first self-published piece of art and writing was called "How to Be an Artist." It was a description of how I intended to live my life each day. It was also the statement of my belief that we are all artists of life, or can be.

How To Be an ARTIST

This piece of art and writing became a best-selling poster and led to the creation of my first book.

I finally dared to create the kind of book I'd dreamed of making so many times. I faced massive self-doubt, ruthless inner critics, and nearly paralyzing fear, but I did it anyway. I literally followed the way of my creative dreams, even when it seemed there was no path.

I HAD NO EXPECTATIONS or hope about this slim little book called *A Creative Companion*, but when I first saw it after it was published, it seemed to me that it glowed in the dark, that the colors vibrated off the page.

I knew then that it would touch many hearts and souls.

I went on to write 11 more books, one each year, and created 20 posters on all sorts of life subjects. I started a company in 1993 to support my creations. I began teaching classes and speaking to groups.

I've been teaching, speaking, and writing about creative dreams for over 15 years, and here is what I've discovered:

85% of people can immediately identify one or more of their creative dreams, without much prompting from me.

The other 15% are just not sure what their dream is, but they'd like to have one.

So I'd like to ask you:

What's your Dream?

Is it small as a dot, or as large as Africa?
Is it immeasurable?

How much of your time is spent living your dream?

When will you begin letting yourself live your dream?

Have you ever pondered any of these questions? How do they make you feel? Maybe they make you want to just lie down and rest because:

"Living one's dream is a big deal and after all, nobody really gets to live theirs, I have enough just as things are, so why even try to live my dream . . ."

"I Don't HAVE TiMe To DreaM!"

Or maybe you're saying inside your round, proud, possibly confused head:

"I've been trying to live my dream and it's really hard and dreams need money and I can't find any and my dream is really just too improbable . . ."

Perhaps your response is as simple as:

"I'm just too busy to stuff one more thing into my head about dreams or anything else! After all, money has got to be made. Doesn't it?" (yes it does)

CreaTive DreaMs Are True and YOURS Are Very IMportanT

and DreaM your little HeaD off

Creative dreams are true and yours are very important

Even if your creative dreams don't, or haven't yet, or never will make money, **they are extremely important.**

OUR DREAMS NEED US and the world needs our dreams.

I believe and know that your willingness and ability to live your creative dreams directly benefits the whole world. Every person living or actively engaged in living his or her dream is more available to be of use to others. When we are consciously expanding ourselves and our dreams, we attract and add to what is needed in this world.

I also know that you have enough of what you need right now to begin living your dream, and I can prove it to you.

Put this book down and imagine your dream. Or if you're already living your dream, picture it getting bigger and richer.

Mmmm . . . . Book is humming while you envision

Did you get a picture of your dream or dreams?

This is proof that your dreams are inside you. This book is a map to making your dreams inside come outside.

If you didn't get an image or picture, that's perfectly O.K. You might not be ready, or images may not come to you visually. If you feel inclined, make a note of your dream.

We'll wait for you...

Do you describe yourself as any of the following:

Busy, procrastinator, perfectionist, avoider, lazy, unstructured, disorganized, unfocused, or resistant?

Excellent.

You can make your creative dreams real even if you describe yourself as all of the above. I know this, because I am often all of the above.

This book will also work well if you've:

Tried everything else, have a short attention span, feel hopeless, or have no money. I have a lot of experience with each of these situations and I can tell you how to work with them.

This book will also help you if you're flying (or bumping) along with your dreams and are seeking support, community, or kindred spirits for your journey.

Creative dreams love to be shared, and whatever dream you have, I can help you find other dreamers nearby.

If you only have the time right now to read this book, or even part of this book, don't worry. Creative dreams are very resilient. Whatever resources you have or don't have, or type of life you're currently living, your dreams glow in the dark even if you don't ever tend to them. They will wait for you. I know this because I wrote my first book at age 10, but I wasn't published until I was 35. My dream waited for me and I have so many more that are still waiting.

Be aware that society is a dream-tester. Your dreams might be shaken, stirred, ignored, copied, disregarded, made fun of, resisted, or squashed.

This is good.

Your willingness to live your dreams must be strengthened and examined. The world will assist you in doing this by bringing you these kinds of challenges.

You might crumble, struggle, fight, give up, or feel crushed. Your creative dreams are untouched by all of this.

Remember:

Dreams are resilient

Other people will probably be against your creative dreams. This is almost for certain, and especially applies to family members who may not have chosen to live their dreams. They might mock you or sarcastically say, as my father used to:

"Dream on, kid!"

This is good news. It means that your creative dreams have been made visible. **Your willingness and choice** to make them even more visible is the whole point of this book. **I wanted to write a book to help all the creative dreamers** make their creative dreams real. I learn and teach lessons daily about being an active creative dreamer and what that actually means.

I have a lot to share about struggle and success, and the l o n g flat places in between. My experiences as a recovering procrastinator and perfectionist give me a keen understanding of how they work to delay creative dreams (and why that's sometimes a good thing). I admit my "splendid imperfections" because I know that my mistakes and stumblings can be of use to others.

I give permission for creative dreamers to do more resting, lying down, and napping, all of which benefits creative dreams. I have suggestions for awakening creative dreams, especially when you think you have no time, energy, or money. I know rejection intimately and can offer new ways to perceive it.

I am endlessly inspired by people's creative dreams. I see the sparkle in their eyes, and

hear their excitement and joy as they share their dreams in groups and gatherings around the country. I am always thrilled when I see the instantly close community that is created when people share their dreams. When I see people avidly supporting each other's creative dreams, I know that this is a deeply powerful force for goodness and change. The world will turn eagerly toward you and your creative dreams if only you can allow yourself the freedom to express them.

I KNOW THAT HELPING to make creative dreams real is my most important work. In a very real sense, my creative dreams have not only saved my life, but have gone on to save and inspire so many other lives.

This is what creative dreams do.

Let this book be your haven, guide, fairy godmother, or map to making your creative dreams real. It's a "paper lantern" to illuminate your path.

This book is indelibly committed to your dreams forever, and it doesn't mind if you feel uncertain, not ready, or convinced of failure. This book comes from my soul to yours, and I've made gigantic mistakes, and spent time ashamed and hiding. I've tried to deny and alter my dreams. I've quit and started and again and I now know that starting is not better than quitting—it's just different. It's a circular dance of quitting and starting over and over again.

Your creative dreams love this book
because they want to be sheltered, nourished, supported, seen, heard, and known.

You might be able to tell that this is not a normal book. This book is inner-active.

Its purpose is to assist you in awakening your inner self.

It is deliberately a little bit crooked, flawed, and intensely optimistic. It will have a hypnotic effect and will adjust itself to your mood and pace. It is also deeply practical, highly effective, and concentrated.

You can even fall asleep and it will work!

There is a "program" in this book, but you do not need to follow the program for it to work.

Your involvement with this book can be highly variable, and you will still notice changes and results.

Just focusing your attention on your creative dreams is a very powerful type of energy. That energy is a renewable source of power for you.

I want to declare that books do not need to be finished to be of value. This book is our dialogue and conversation about living our creative dreams. It is an ongoing conversation without end. You can dip into this book, gobble it up, do all the things it suggests, explore every resource, game, and invention, or just lie quietly, smiling at the cover.

It will smile back.

Guide to Using This Book

MY INTENTION IS THAT THIS BE A BOOK that fits in with your real life—not an idealized version of it. That's why I'm inviting all of us who are busy, avoiding, practicing procrastinators and perfectionists, and people who really would rather sleep all day, to participate.

I have made a 12-month "program" or path to living your creative dreams. Within each month, there is a step for each week of the year. You can follow these steps in order, or you can start in the middle, or with any section that speaks particularly to you. Use increments of time that serve you best. You might take 12 months, 12 weeks, or 12 years with this material. There is no "right way."

Each month also has a game, a gift, a challenge, and resources at the end.

My intention is to inspire you to discover your creative dreams, or if they're already moving, ways to nourish them, and you, with plenty of fresh ideas and love.

I created two kinds of tables of contents:

1. THIS IS FOR PEOPLE who are thrilled by logic and the linear world. It is in the form of a list, a program, and a method.

2. THIS IS FOR PEOPLE who are delighted by the abstract, nonlinear, or visual. It is in the form of a game, a map, or a path.

Both styles may serve you, or just one may suffice. Choose according to what pleases you, or experiment with both!

I'd like to extend a personal invitation to you to visit my websight, **www.planetsark.com,** and find additional resources and a community to support your creative dreams and creative dream-living. In order to accelerate our creative dreams and make them real, we need the support of a creative community. Please consider yourself a part of this community.

In this book . . .

You'll find many books and websights recommended by me at the end of each chapter. These are all books I've read and worked with, and the websights are ones that I visit regularly. It is an eccentric list that is limited only by the amount of space in the book. If you'd like to see more of my book recommendations, they are in my previous 11 books.

Please feel free to color or draw in this book if it's your own copy. I know we are all taught not to, especially in a hardcover book, but I am encouraging you to creatively change the pages of your own book (besides, I'd love to see your pages if we meet).

Table of Contents #1
For those more gifted in the linear realms

1. Fantastic First Month
Finding and Naming Your Dream(s) 24

THE PURPOSE OF THIS CHAPTER is to assist you in choosing a dream (or dreams) or to strengthen the one(s) you already have.

2. Succulent Second Month
The Land of No 42

THE PURPOSE OF THIS CHAPTER is to explore and remove blocks that prevent you from living your dreams. It answers the question, "What stops you?"

3. Treasured Third Month
The World of Yes 67

THE PURPOSE OF THIS CHAPTER is to identify all the reasons you can and will live your creative dreams. It answers the question, "What starts you?"

4. Feisty Fourth Month
Making Creative Dreams Real with MicroMOVEments 88

THE PURPOSE OF THIS CHAPTER is to learn and practice the micromovement method, which works even if you don't want to.

5. Fabulous Fifth Month
Creative Dreams Support Systems 105

THE PURPOSE OF THIS CHAPTER is to assist you in building or adding to your support system, and reminding you that you are not alone.

6. Sublime Sixth Month
Committing to Your Dream and Keeping It Moving 124

THE PURPOSE OF THIS CHAPTER is to strengthen your commitment to your creative dream and find out more about time and what keeps dreams moving.

7. Superb Seventh Month

Inspiring Stories and Examples of Creative Dreams and Dreamers 141

THE PURPOSE OF THIS CHAPTER is to connect you with other people and their creative dream experiences. This gives you a virtual dream community to inspire your creative dreams.

8. Ecstatic Eighth Month

Living Your Creative Dreams 169

THE PURPOSE OF THIS CHAPTER is to deal with the difficult parts of actually living your creative dreams.

9. Nourishing Ninth Month

Nourishing You and Your Creative Dreams 187

THE PURPOSE OF THIS CHAPTER is to refresh you and your creative dreams, and to assist you if you feel stuck.

10. Terrific Tenth Month
What You and Your Dreams Need Now 205

THE PURPOSE OF THIS CHAPTER is to discover what stage your dream is at and where it needs to go or grow.

11. Energizing
Eleventh Month
Managing and Growing Your Creative Dreams 226

THE PURPOSE OF THIS CHAPTER is to learn about management and growth of your creative dreams.

Dream Stoppers 244

QUICK REFERENCE FOR WHAT STOPS YOU

Dream Starters 245

QUICK REFERENCE FOR WHAT STARTS YOU

12. Tender Twelfth Month
Living Elegantly and Successfully with Your Creative Dreams 250

THE PURPOSE OF THIS CHAPTER is to support and encourage a healthy model of success and celebration with regard to your creative dreams.

CHAPTER ONE

Fantastic
First Month

Finding and Naming Your Dream(s)

The purpose of this chapter is to assist you in choosing a dream (or dreams) or to strengthen the one(s) you already have.

What's Your Dream?

FIRST, I WANT TO WRAP YOU IN A CLOAK OF COMFORT AND SAFETY. Comfort coaxes dreams out. You can get some paper and markers for this next part because notes or drawings can be helpful in this process. Or, if you wish, just read along and imagine that you're writing or drawing.

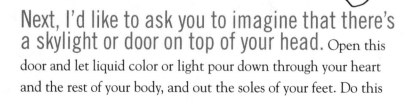

your
DrEAM
cloAk

Next, I'd like to ask you to imagine that there's a skylight or door on top of your head. Open this door and let liquid color or light pour down through your heart and the rest of your body, and out the soles of your feet. Do this several times, until you feel more space inside. Let this transform your energy and expand it. You might find yourself smiling slightly, or grinning.

now, take a deep breath

WE FORGET TO BREATHE CONSCIOUSLY, or to honor our progress with a celebratory breath.

Let this deep breath lead you into imagining or picturing your dream.

If you already know what your dream is, just make a note of it, and then if you wish, come along to explore new dreams.

If you don't know what your dream is, or aren't sure, I'd like to invite you to create a dream activator inside yourself. If you are reading these words, you have already done this! This is a state of mind that is curious, flexible, and ready to make decisions. Let the dream activator bring you back to the first page of the book, where you will reread the creative dream description. Next, go to pages 34, 35 and read through the dream categories.

Now, what creative dream can you imagine doing?

Let the dream activator work on your behalf to choose one.

Write it down, or have it in mind.

you can Always cHange it...

If you still don't know, or aren't ready to choose, that's O.K., because the dream activator will work as you read this book. I'm a recovering perfectionist who is often afraid to "choose the wrong thing," so I don't choose anything, thinking that will keep me safe. Safe from what? Safe from playing a game in a book that might bring more light into my life?

How Living Your Dreams Benefits You and Others

DO YOU SPARKLE? Is there a certain glint in your smile? Is there a time in your day or night that belongs to no one but you, where you do something you love?

When someone asks, "Are you doing what you love? Are you living your dreams?" can you answer with a resounding yes? If not, are you in a process of discovering what your dreams are?

People living their dreams are more joy-full and full of life.

You can tell when you meet them because you feel refreshed or uplifted by their presence. This joy carries over into everything they do. To creative dream-livers, the world is full of opportunities, adventures, and chances to think and act creatively. A "dream liver" is more likely to think of new ways to overcome challenges in life.

When you are fully, or partially, engaged in living your dreams, you actually create more energy. This energy can then be used to help others in creative and interesting ways.

PEOPLE WHO FEEL STIFLED or bored by their work, or blocked or repressed about their creative dreams, will barely have enough energy to function in their own lives, and not much or none to act on the behalf of others.

IT IS CLEAR that the living of creative dreams directly benefits the world and everyone in it.

We need more encouragement and education for creative dreams.

"Never doubt that a small group of committed citizens can change the world. Indeed, it's the only thing that ever has." —Margaret Mead

SCHOOLS AND BUSINESSES need to nurture and support the living of creative dreams. This is precisely why we need continued arts education in schools.

I dream of newspapers that cover news of creative dreams at various stages. I dream of businesses that establish charitable funds for arts education groups.

WE DON'T NEED TO WAIT for newspapers and businesses to change—we can establish these things ourselves. If you bought this book, you are already taking action.

We are all artists and creative dreamers. Society would have us believe that only some of us are.

The world will benefit immensely from more people living their dreams. These people will be able to offer solutions and creative thought to long-standing problems and challenges. Active dream-living directly feeds creativity and fresh thinking. We need more fresh thinking!

Everyone loves a dream

We Are All energiZed By creative DreAMS

People love to be near or involved with dreams and the living of dreams. Dream-livers create a community wherever they go. It is natural to be energized and enthused about dreams. Doing and being what we love is what we were born to do.

We came here to live our dreams.

Who Dreams?

"Ordinary people" are living their dreams every day. These ordinary souls sparkle on the inside and maybe also on the outside. These people have chosen to live their dreams and spend parts of their days and nights engaged in doing something they love. Even more than doing, they are being their dreams.

They're sitting on the bus, pushing a baby stroller, stocking groceries. You can still have a "regular job" and live your dreams.

Let your "regular job" support your dreams.

TALKING ABOUT DREAMS is very important. People love to share their dreams, and this promotes dream expansion.

We are meant to expand our dreams and our visions.

Why Dream?

Life is a difficult assignment. We are fragile creatures, expected to function at high rates of speed, and asked to accomplish great and small things each day. These daily activities take enormous amounts of energy. Most things are out of our control. We are surrounded by danger, frustration, grief, and insanity as well as love, hope, ecstasy, and wonder. Being fully human is an exercise in humility, suffering, grace, and great humor. Things and people all around us die, get broken, or are lost. There is no safety or guarantees.

THE WAY TO ACCOMPLISH the assignment of truly living is to engage fully, richly, and deeply in the living of your dreams. We are made to dream and to live those dreams!

WE ARE SUCCULENT, FLEXIBLE, INGENIOUS CREATURES, gifted with great intelligence, enormous resources, and endless creativity. We are all mentored in our dreams by our ancestors. Our dreams sustain and support us, even when we're not actively living them. They infuse us with a hope and certainty. Every person living his or her dream is better able to help the world and other people not yet living their dreams.

Let's explore.

Remembering Dreams

"I always wanted to _____
_____."

"I used to think I could_____
_____."

Make notes *or imagine that you are.*

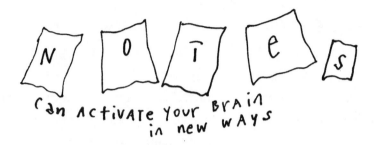

NOTES can Activate your Brain in new ways

Your answers to these questions may flood you with reasons you can't do or live your dream(s). This is to be expected. Our minds try to protect us from any large or small change, including increased happiness—especially increased happiness. Our minds perceive even happiness as a threat to our accustomed struggle.

"If I really lived my dream, I might need to _____
_____."

Choose one of the words/phrases below, or make up one of your own.

> change
> advance
> grow
> do something different
> live in a new way

"If I _____, I might need to _____."

> revise my thinking
> quit my job
> stop complaining
> figure out a new way
> change something

THESE HIDDEN THOUGHTS RUN OUR LIVES. See if you can get to the deepest reason that you might not be living your dream. See if it applies to new or unfamiliar dreams you might have.

"If I lived my dream, I would be _____

_____."

Here are some typical thoughts you might have:
expected to be happy all the time
unable to keep struggling and complaining
so busy that I couldn't stand it
pressured to succeed
challenged by the unknown

What are you doing instead of living your dreams?

1. working
2. sleeping
3. eating
4.
5.
6.
7.
8.

What if you added living your dreams to your list? What would that mean?

If you are already living your dream, would you like to dedicate more time or energy to it? What would that mean?

Many dreams are undercover

DO YOU HAVE DREAMS IN A DRAWER? Or a closet? Are there dreams inside your computer? People put dreams in boxes or in storage.

I'll get this
out later
when I have
more time

Guess what?

MANY
DRAWERS
ARE
BULGING
WITH
DREAMS

More time never comes
Time flows naturally to what is

visible

active

important

necessary

You can make your dreams visible, active, important, and necessary

Liberate your dream(s) from any "holding place" or hiding place. You can do this by physically moving your dream from one place to another. Is there something you can move right now?
We'll wait.

If you are paralyzed by inertia, I will show you a simple way to create movement in chapter 4.

Dreams want to come out and play

Your Dream Legacy

Many of us had dreams as children or young adults that might have gotten lost, blocked, or stifled in some way. That dream may have changed, but the process of remembering it is important. It may have seeds for your dreams now.

Let Me Ask You:
Answer from the viewpoint of a 7- to 10-year-old

Who was your best friend?

What was your favorite thing to eat?

Where was your favorite spot in the house?

Where was your favorite spot outside the house?

What did you dream about doing or being?

SEE IF ANY ANSWERS COME, even if the answer doesn't seem to make sense right now. You can use your nondominant hand if you wish. It's a way for inner children to speak.

I feel like I'm still the **wake-up fairy** today (which was my first job in kindergarten) as an author and artist (I just have a bigger magic wand).

If no answers come, that's perfectly O.K. Set this aside for now and see what your sleeping dreams might reveal.

MY MAGIC WAND WAKES UP creAtive sPirits

Were your dreams encouraged?
Discouraged?
How?

Did your parents or caregivers identify and speak of their dream? Can you recall what they were?

Did your parents' choices about their dreams influence your dream choices? How?

Are you supportive of children's dreams (your children or others')?

Are you supportive of your dream(s)? How?

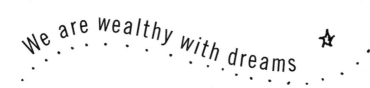

We are wealthy with dreams

The intention to and belief in living a dream is absolutely free.

The living of that dream can cost money, time, and energy. What are you willing to invest in your dream(s)?

Naming Your Dream
Identifying Your Dream

Some people can easily identify one primary dream. For others, a dream is more elusive. These people often have many dreams at once, or a general idea of a dream that never takes a specific shape.

Dreams respond well to specific descriptions and become more real when you can name them.

Maybe you can find your dream in the following categories:

DREAMS OF SERVICE

Making your contribution by giving to others.

You can do this in the following ways:

    Practicing medicine

    Teaching

    Working for nonprofit organizations

    Joining environmental causes

    Practicing psychology

    Devoting yourself to meditation or religion

DREAMS OF THE ARTS

Using the arts as a channel for your creativity.

You can do this in the following ways:

    Writing and publishing

    Dancing

    Performing in the theater (or outside of it)

    Public speaking

    Painting or drawing

DREAMS OF FAMILY

Making a contribution through family systems.

You can do this in the following ways:

    Providing child care

    Giving birth or adopting

    Providing foster care

    Providing elder care

DREAMS OF SELF-EXPLORATION

Making a contribution through self-knowledge.

You can do this in the following ways:

    Traveling

    Donating time or experience

    Living outside your own culture

    Experimenting with different occupations

You cannot choose the wrong dream

If you do, you'll be able to tell because it will feel flat and stale and have no life of its own.

I think that there are more fears about choosing dreams than there is lack of dreams.

What's your dream?

If you're not able to be specific, can you choose a general theme?

"I want to _____

_____."

help people

build or create something new

find a new way to live my dreams

choose what seems like a dream

You can build your dream choice within this book

Let's look at the different stages of dream development:

Stages of Dream Development

A JUST- HATCHED DreAM needs special cAre

I discovered that making your creative dream real happens in seven clearly identifiable stages that duplicate our growth as humans.

1. Egg: Idea, beginning, tiny thought.

2. Hatched: Idea born, made visible, tangible, physical.

3. Infant or baby: Creative dream in its infancy. Needs a lot of shelter, care, and protection.

4. Toddler: Your creative dream is very demanding of your time and attention and can be charming and endearing

5. Child: You have a routine with your creative dream. It feeds you, you feed it, you are becoming interdependent.

6. Adolescent: Your creative dream rebels and also challenges you in different ways.

7. Adult: Your creative dream can live on its own without you. You are interdependent and integrated.

You may have a number of dreams in different stages of growth. It is good to pay attention to how many baby dreams you are feeding and sheltering!

See if you can locate what stage your creative dream is at.

Fantastic First Month

Finding and Naming Your Dreams

☆
week one

A Game or Something to Try

Note: it isn't necessary to try these things to be "doing this book." Sometimes just reading one thing will create new pathways in your mind, a little more space, a tiny grin, a quick flash of recognition. These things will also serve your dream-making.

Get a blank book, journal, or pieces of paper tied by string.
Write a title and your name on the cover.
Here are some suggestions for other pages in your guidebook:

1. **Your creative dream(s)** write one, or some. Down here
2. **What stops you?** List things that make you quit
3. **What starts you?** List things that make you begin and continue
4. **Who supports and inspires you?** List and describe them
5. **Choose a micro-movement** Tiny little movement (see chapter) 4
6. **Resources** List books and websights and phone numbers

You are the best author of your own guidebook...

Lie Down IMMEDIATELY

Most of us are overwhelmed or tired. We cannot apply creative thinking when we're tired. Even 5 minutes of lying down will change your brain chemistry and open new patterns of thought.

Create Your Own Guidebook of Creative Dreams

You can use a blank book or just blank paper clipped together. Put photographs or scraps from magazines in it that represent your creative dreams. Draw, scribble, or paint in between the images. Make a list of creative dreams you've thought of or admire in others.

You can use your book lots of other times in upcoming chapters.

A G I F T for You

This imaginary gift is a journey for your imagination. It is a resting place within this book and will inspire you to travel inside your mind to brand-new places. I invite you to lie down and just let the images in. This will energize and relax your creative mind.

I SEND YOU . . .

A luxury train ride. On this train are all the inspiring people you've ever wanted to meet or talk to. You glide from car to car, sitting or lying down on velvet lounge chairs, listening and asking questions. There is also a voluminous library on the train, with every book you've ever wanted to read or look at. Kind people bring you delicious tidbits to eat and nourishing liquids to drink. If you take a nap, time stands still until you return so you never miss anything. You receive a large journal filled with photographs, drawings and descriptions of your journey to take with you when you leave. You realize that you can board this train at any time.

week three

A Positive Challenge (I Dare You)

Ask one friend . . .

To be your listener, your "compassionate witness" for your creative dream(s). Explain that you don't need solutions or motivation right now, just someone to listen and witness as you move through your process.

Describe your creative dream(s) as fully as you can and with as much detail as possible, and take your time doing it.

If you have difficulty asking for or receiving this kind of attention (most of us do!) think of some things you could offer in exchange.

week four

RADIANT Resources

A Big New Free Happy Unusual Life: Self-Expression and Spiritual Practice for Those Who Have Time for Neither
  Nina Wise

A Creative Companion: How to Free Your Creative Spirit
  SARK

Life Drawing Life
  Frederick Franck

The Right to Write: An Invitation and Initiation into the Writing Life
  Julia Cameron

Energy Medicine
  Donna Eden

Fingerpainting on the Moon: Writing and Creativity As a Path to Freedom
  Peter Levitt

Traveling Light (only available at www.storypeople.com)
www.peoplewhodare.com
www.storypeople.com
www.cherylrichardson.com
www.marcallen.com

MOVIE: *Beautiful Dreamers*
  directed by John Kent Harrison

CHAPTER TWO

Succulent
Second Month

The Land of No

All the reasons you can't or haven't been living your dreams

The purpose of this chapter is to explore and remove blocks that prevent you from living your dreams. It answers the question, "What stops you?"

IMAGINE A DARK LAND FULL OF BARBED WIRE FENCES, no trespassing signs, and unfinished roads leading to nowhere. The land is unwelcoming in every way. Yet many of us live there. It is the Land of No. There are no creative dreams here!

These are not healthy, consciously considered "nos," but automatic answers to every question. Most of us have a part of our mind like this Land of No. But the Land of No is actually all just a dark facade. Grab a flashlight and let's go exploring.

Fear and Negativity

WHEN WE THINK OF LIVING OUR CREATIVE DREAMS, many of us become afraid. Our main fear is usually that we'll fail. Of course, the real failure is in not trying, but fear hypnotizes us into forgetting that. Fear's job is to make sure we don't try . . . Then we'll be

SAFE
Safe and small and not dreaming at all

Fears like to live undisturbed in our heads. Fears love to crowd into our heads and take up all the space. They make a cacophony of discordant sounds:

"What if I try it, and it doesn't work?"

"Oh, what's the use—it's too late now."

"This is a stupid idea."

"I just don't have time (money, space) to dream."

Here's a way to change that. Get a scrap or sheet of paper. Make a fast list of every fear you can think of that keeps you from living your creative dream(s).

"reality is merely an illusion, albeit a very persistent one." Albert einstein

Here's one of my lists:

i'll never have enough time
too scary
i don't know how
How will I ever stop being overwhelmed
it's really hard
WHAT WHERE will i find enough HELP?

Tearing into little pieces feels very liberating and gives your Brain A rest

Now, read through the list, and then tear it into as many pieces as you can. The fears are now separate from you (or out of your head and onto paper) and just for those few seconds there is a spaciousness inside your beautiful brain. Feel this spaciousness.

We can meet our fears in a new way with a fresh mind and a full heart. We can learn to listen more briefly to our fears, and escort them out into the garden while we have a tea party in the living room. We can study our fears objectively, like we would study a subject in school. We can retrain our minds.

Negative thinking ☆

THERE IS A LOT OF SUPPORT IN OUR SOCIETY FOR NEGATIVE THINKING. It is easy to be critical, find fault, and focus on negativity, because it seems like you are doing something. It can also feel familiar and curiously safe. "Well, I'm glad I didn't go too far with that cockamamy idea . . ."

Negative thinking patterns are creative dream repellents. Whatever creative dream you might think of, negative thinking can squash it flat.

You might share your creative dream with someone and fall into his or her negative thinking pattern. "Gee, have you really thought this through? I've heard terrible things about . . ." We are all tempted to lay our templates of the past onto the present. Everything negative we've heard and experienced is a candidate for negative thinking recycling. Negative thinking is not the same as caution or a considered choice. Negative thinking does not protect you or others.

Negative thinking isn't intrinsically bad—it's just a habitual form of contraction.

Creative dreams need expansion—negative thinking is a contraction.

We can learn about our negative patterns, be aware of them, and choose different ways of thinking.

Here's Something to Try:

Write 3 negative statements about this creative dream:

Being a Painter

1. "It is very difficult to get started in the fine arts—especially after a certain age."

2. "Painting talent is just something you're born with—no use in trying to develop it."

3. "Most galleries won't waste their time looking at emerging painters."

Let's reframe each of these statements:

1. "It's easy for people of all ages to get started in the fine arts."

2. "It is exciting to find ways to develop our talents as artists."

3. "There are lots of galleries eager to find new painters."

How does your body feel when you read these statements?

It doesn't really matter if you believe the reframed statements or not. In fact, if you're a habitual negative thinker, you won't believe them. The thing to do is to practice reframing until *it* becomes the habit and not the negativity.

If you practice thinking differently, you will begin to have experiences that reflect your new way of thinking. The negative thinker attracts exactly what he or she predicts.

You could describe this as "positive thinking," but I think that the phrase is overused and slightly annoying somehow.

Procrastination and Perfectionism ☆

Procrastinators and/or Perfectionists

(85% of us are) If you're not either of these, please reach out to someone who is and share your expertise.

Just read this later . . .

"Later" is the favorite word of procrastinators, and it isn't because they're lazy. Most procrastinators are also perfectionists. This is a neat trick because it means that most things don't get started (procrastination) and most things don't get finished (perfectionism).

Creative dreams are big assignments and procrastinators/
perfectionists are prone to assign themselves HUGE goals
that turn out to feel impossible to reach.

Initially, the goal or dream is exciting and marvelous:

I'm going to be a famous writer

SOMEHOW, TEN YEARS PASS before any words actually make it
onto the paper. But the procrastinator is happily writing in his or
her head, rehearsing future book signings, imagining how he or
she will autograph the book.

This all takes place without ever actually moving or physically
manifesting much (or any) of the creative dream. When it comes
time to actually write, the procrastinator/perfectionist is too tired
from all of the thinking he's been doing and he needs to rest up
so he can do more thinking about it!

Here's the deal:

Procrastination works as a creative dream-stopper. Sometimes we simply need more time, and

procrastination works beautifully for this. These are what I call
the "gifts of procrastination." The other gift is that we can remain
unjudged. Procrastination is mostly a habit of not completing
physically. Procrastination also lets us "dream without action,"
which is sometimes useful for the discovery processes (giving us
time . . .).

The problem with procrastination as it relates to creative
dreams is that it is a habit that gets stronger as it gets reinforced.

We can learn new habits of completion.

Procrastination is all about doing things later. Later rarely turns
into now, and creative dreams keep waiting for our attention.
Procrastinators also love to burst into activity with huge
declarations.

"I'm going to write for 4 to 6 hours daily!"

Which lasts for a day or maybe two (or even a month), and then real life enters in and the procrastinator retreats back into his mind where the message is: "See! You never finish anything . . ." (There is a simple remedy for this in chapter 4.)

Perfectionism ☆

The main phrase for the perfectionist is "not yet"

THIS IS BECAUSE IT'S NEVER QUITE GOOD ENOUGH, or ready, or perfect as the perfectionist has imagined it. The perfectionist is constantly fine tuning, redoing, shaping, polishing, getting ready, adjusting, tinkering . . .

The perfectionist will share his or her work with others with huge explanations:

"Oh, this will have more definition."

"Once I finish this, it will look much better."

"This side will have a lot more glitter and a row of buttons and a bow on top too!"

And at the slightest perceived comment or perceived criticism he or she will retreat back.

"See! I knew it wasn't yet time to share it."

So, back to the drawing board, which could go on for years, until it's time again to try sharing whatever it is.

Perfectionism is not about making it better; it's about not making it at all.

Perfectionism is what stops many people from sharing their creative dreams, ideas, or reality with others.

Perfectionists have unbelievably high standards to which they compare themselves and their creative dreams. Even a mild case of perfectionism can cause this.

The blessings of perfectionism are that the work is often uncommonly good, if the perfectionist can just get brave or determined enough to share with a sensitive and insightful person.

We will be working with procrastination and perfectionism throughout this book.

Resistance and Inertia

RESISTANCE IS THE FULL-STOP METHOD FOR CREATIVE DREAMING. The words for this are:

opposing

refusal

Resistance often gets activated when we've begun exploring a creative dream, encountered fear and engaged in negative thinking, and observed ourselves to be procrastinating or practicing perfectionism.

The underlying message of resistance is "What's the use? It will never work anyway."

We have giant examples of why it will never work, and resistance seems easiest and best.

The gifts of resistance are that sometimes we need to quit before we can really begin. Sometimes our own resistance can act as an antidote to resisting!

Resistance is also sneaky and can show up as apathy or exhaustion. "Oh, I tried a lot of things already and it looks like it just isn't going to work."

If we explore this resistance, we may find that the person made three phone calls or sent out eight letters and then turned resistant to any further effort.

A creative dream will test your opposition and your refusal by taking you through every chance to do both.

Try this.

Take a creative dream: Being a filmmaker

(or use your own) and list three things you are resisting doing with this dream.

For example:

> showing the film I made to more people
>
> buying a better video camera
>
> making time to write down my ideas

Then ask, what else am I resisting doing? Are you resisting doing new things? And if you've been making progress, are you resisting fully accepting that you have done new things about your creative dream?

See if you can identify it or what you're resisting and at least choose to resist (or not).

Often resistance feels like an unscalable wall, when there are actually footholds all over the place.

Inertia ☆

INERTIA IS THE TENDENCY OF ANY MATERIAL BODY to maintain its velocity indefinitely unless accelerated or decelerated by some force.

Inertia is a form of paralysis. It just feels insurmountable. The phrases for inertia are, "Oh, why bother? It's too much." Creative dreams can stay in a state of inertia for many, many years. Inertia would have us believe that we've done enough.

The gift of inertia is the absence of movement. "Oh, thank heavens. I don't need to do anything right now." Then you can go back to doing nothing.

The challenge of inertia is that absence of movement can continue long after we'd actually like to be moving.

Try this: Ask yourself about inertia and how or if you experience it. Did you choose inertia? Did you choose inertia about your creative dream for this amount of time? Inertia can settle over us like a thick blanket. We may not even recognize it as inertia.

Here's how you can tell if you wish to do something with a creative dream and you've already explored fear, resistance, procrastination, and perfectionism. If you're still not moving, it's probably inertia.

Antidotes for the inertia bound are

Movements of any kind about anything

The tiniest movement can break the spell of inertia. Taking out the garbage or making the bed can shift your energy.

Staying in the inertia until it becomes impossibly boring

This can take quite a while, but usually, eventually, works.

Learning to know when inertia is upon you

You can do this by noticing your particular signs of inertia, like quitting, hiding, or feeling frozen and unable to do anything.

Inside Critics

THE CRITICAL VOICES in our own heads are far more vicious than what we might hear from the outside. Our "inside critics" have intimate knowledge of us and can zero in on our weakest spots.

In relation to creative dreams, the inside critics might say:

Ha! Fat chance.

Remember when you tried _____ and it flopped?

You are a middle-aged person/a young person/an old person, how do you expect to _____ ?

You don't have the money to be fooling around like this.

You might be told by the critics that you're too fat, too old, too young, not intelligent enough, a quitter, not logical, prone to try too many things . . .

It's all balderdash!

Some elements of these may be true, and it's completely up to you how they affect you. Inside critics are really just trying to protect you. You can:

Learn to dialogue with them (see resources at end of this section).

Give them new jobs.

Turn them into allies.

You can also dismantle them/exterminate them.

Here's something to try:

Draw a picture of one of your inside critics, then tear it up with great drama. Inside critics do not know more than we do—it can just appear that way.

i HAve A GanG of critics THAT ofTen AppeAr As "inner Bullies" i Am leArninG To Trans·Form THeir enerGy

Here are a few things to try:

Study inner critics from reading books and listening to tapes by Hal and Sidra Stone.

Learn to recognize when you're under an inner critic attack. You will feel incredibly negative and hopeless.

Reassign your inner critics and invent creative new jobs for them. I sent mine on an expedition to Madagascar, searching for rare lemurs!

Stop your inner critics by not listening or engaging with them at all.

Begin to discover the process of turning your critics into allies.

Dismiss them from the rest of this book!

"Inside" Children

INSIDE EACH OF US ARE THE CHILDREN we were at each developmental stage. I've discovered the following ages inside myself: infant, 2, 4, 7, 10, 13, 16, 18, 21. As we progress through life, different-aged children become activated by the circumstances and choices of our lives.

With regard to our creative dreams, these inside children can prevent us from living them by "acting out" in order to try to get out attention. Your inner 5-year-old is not going to patiently wait as you learn intricate metalworking techniques or study impressionist painting. Yet, your inner 10-year-old may be perfectly suited to learn and observe new skills.

What's really needed is parenting of these inside children so that we bring them to age-appropriate activities.

Creative dreams take time and energy, and so do inside children. Unparented inside children are certain to affect your creative dreams. Well-parented inside children can be of great benefit.

Here are a few things to try:

Locate your "inside parent." You can do this by picturing yourself as your most nurturing, kind and loving self.

Locate an "inside child."

You can do this by visualizing or meditating about a younger version of yourself. Ask this young person to communicate with you. You might communicate by:

Drawing or writing. Let your nondominant hand write what you imagine your child would say.

Listening. What is your inside child saying?

Seeing. Picture yourself at a younger age. What do you see?

Ask an inside child to contribute to your creative dream-making.

Choose an appropriate activity and ask for assistance from that inside child. The assistance might come in the form of unexpected insights or brand-new ideas.

Learn to be a parent to your own inside children.

You can do this by studying the subject of inner children. There are books, tapes, and workshops to learn from. Your creative dreams will grow and expand due to your new relationship to the "kids" inside you.

Grudge Island

THIS IS A PLACE WHERE EVERYONE wears backpacks loaded with grudges and sifts through them to discuss:

"What could have happened if only . . ."

"I can prove I was right!"

Our creative dreams are subject to grudge-holding when we decide that other people somehow have made their dreams real and we have not.

It is common for people to hold these grudges against parents, teachers, and schools for years. Spouses are another typical area for grudge-holding.

"If he/she had been home more, was supportive of my dreams . . ."

"If we had money for me to attend classes."

"I was so busy with _____ that I never had time for _____."

Grudges are often layered or stacked together.

"Because I never had a supportive home/family/parent, I ended up marrying a person just like that and have never taken time for myself or my dreams."

Grudges are the perfect excuse to not fulfill creative dreams. We can blame someone or something else and never take responsibility for our own part in not living our creative dreams.

Along with other types of victim mentality, there is a societal support for grudge-holding.

"Oh my dear, with that background, I can see why you've never been able to _____ or _____."

If you need or want more time to explore your creative dreams, grudges will work well to slow you down or stop you.

If you've had enough of grudge-holding or comparing your dream to someone else's, you can move swiftly to get off Grudge Island and stop spending time with grudges.

Here are a few things to try:

Practice the art of forgiveness. Grudges melt with forgiveness.

List every grudge you can identify. Get them outside of you and look closely at them.

See if you can identify how/if your creative dreams have been affected by grudges or grudge-holding.

Recognize that you can choose differently.

Jealousy and Competition

WITH EVERY CREATIVE DREAM, there can be a fear or concern that someone else has or is already doing it, or doing it better than you.

Creative dreams are not sheltered from that type of thinking, and it is extremely common to feel envious, jealous, or competitive with others about their creative dreams.

IT IS NOT NECESSARILY FAIR whose dream gets attention. There is not a route to follow to ensure that your creative dream will be well received or received at all. There will be people all your life whose creative dreams will be recognized, paid tribute to, and encouraged.

Your creative dreams may be unsung, unseen, or unsupported.

You may open a magazine or watch a TV show and see someone who appears to be living your dream. This may make your creative dream seem smaller or less significant, or like your chances for "success" are somehow being used up. You may feel hostile or territorial or embarrassingly envious of another's creative dream. These feelings are all normal and are not discussed often enough.

Here are some things to think about:

How and when the spotlight shines on someone and his or her creative dream is not necessarily fair, nor is it up to you.

Jealousy/envy that goes unexpressed can cause huge resentments and blocks to living your creative dreams.

Whoever is receiving attention for her creative dreams has her own dealings with jealousy, envy, and competition.

While creative dreams may be the same or similar, the person dreaming them is distinctly unique and one of a kind.

Try these things.

From the Land of No

All of these are useful to visit, just don't stay too long

These words and phrases are commonly used in the Land of No. It is tempting to spend a lot of time here, going over and over "What's not fair" and "How I haven't started living my dreams because . . ."

Below you will find words and phrases from the Land of No and antidotes for increased acceptance of these states of mind.

1. Blame

This includes blaming parents, schools, religion, poverty, world crisis, economy, siblings, and therapists. Mostly it means blaming the self for not living dreams.

antidote for blame:

Blame everyone! Make a massive list. I once made a list of men I blamed on a 50-foot roll of butcher paper. I wrote until I fell asleep sobbing and the marker colors smeared together and got all over me. Then there was more room for my creative dream.

Releasing the blame is the key.

A B s e n c e
H o f p e
  o
is PArALyZiaG

2. Hopeless

"Oh, what's the use?" Absence of hope creates a vacuum that even creative dreams cannot fill.

antidote for feeling hopeless:

Who/what is hopeless? Are you quite certain that you or your dreams are hopeless? Have you spent enough time being hopeless? How much experience have you had in feeling/being hope-full? Draw or write your hopeless story. See if you can draw or write a hope-full story, especially about your creative dream.

Exploring/letting light into hopelessness is the key.

3. Lost

Not knowing who we are, what to do next, floundering, fumbling, so lost that creative dreams cannot be found.

antidote for feeling lost:

Way to behave when we are lost: Stop moving. Drink water, breathe, and consult a map, compass, or refer to landmarks.

Sometimes feeling lost can cause us to become frantic. If we are too frantic, we cannot possibly be active in our creative dream. If you feel lost in regard to your creative dream, it's probably time to consult: a friend, coach, an oracle, a group, or just yourself and a pad of paper. Draw your own map and your own path out.

Consider paths to new places you haven't visited before.

Navigating through lost feelings is the key.

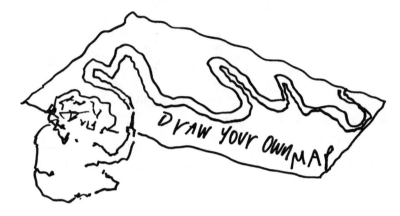

4. Bitter

"Other people are living their dreams, and I'm not and I hate them." Bitterness is a sour outlook that taints our vision and blocks creative dream-making.

antidote for feeling bitter:

Things that are bitter taste sour. Is your bitterness/sourness helping you in some way? Consult your bitter feelings, express them, let them out. Write a bitter letter, make a bitter list. Keep a tiny notebook for your bitter thoughts. It is not better not to be bitter unless you've delved into your bitterness and expressed it in some way. Your creative dream can benefit from your bitterness if you acknowledge it.

Expression and release of bitterness are the keys.

5. Angry

"I am so angry that I feel _____."

Anger at self and others about creative dreams is common.

antidote for anger:

Anger is a great motivator. Anger can propel us in our creative dream-making. Many of us repress our anger, or only let it out in intellectual ways, after the angry feelings have passed.
Experiment with release/expression of anger when you feel it. Even tiny moments toward anger expression can have a big effect. Or you can experiment with meditation or journaling about your anger.

Some of my favorites:
Smashing physical objects, shouting, talking with a trusted friend

Transforming by action or reflection is the key.

6. Overwhelmed

"There is just so much to do! How can I ever make a difference, I am so tired . . ."

antidote for feeling overwhelmed:

Whenever you feel overwhelmed, search for what would take the pressure off. Often when we're overwhelmed, we're assigning everything equal importance. This is an illusion. If you're not able to prioritize, ask a friend to listen to what you are overwhelmed by, and help you to list what's most important.

Moving and changing priorities and taking the pressure off are the keys.

7. Unsupported

"I am always doing everything; how can my creative dreams grow if I'm all by myself?"

antidote for feeling unsupported:

We become hypnotized by isolation, and think we're doing it all by ourselves. Our self-supporting skills are not developed, so when people cancel or disappoint us, we can feel a lack of support. Support is usually very close by, and we haven't learned how or when to ask for it. This can all be changed by studying and practicing new ways of giving and receiving support.

Study and practice are the keys.

8. Misunderstood

"No one understands how important my creative dreams are . . ."

antidote for feeling misunderstood:

Do you feel understood by others? Why or why not?

When we feel misunderstood by other people, it's usually because we haven't given them enough information. Try explaining how you feel and giving other people a chance to understand you.

Clarification and information are the keys.

9. Resistant

"I don't have enough: money, time, energy, resources, etc. I quit. I've put in enough."

antidote for feeling resistant:

Usually when we are resisting something, it is due to fear of some kind. See if you can uncover what fear is causing you to resist, and name it. Now, see if the resistance is still necessary. If it is, let it be your choice and not a reaction to or against something.

Uncovering is the key.

10. Victim dependent

"My creative dreams would be much further along if only I didn't get sidetracked by_____, or have to _____."

antidote for being victim dependent:

Victim thinking is common and painful. It is also a good escape. When you are a victim, nothing is your fault and not much is expected of you. Since every victim needs an oppressor, see if you can discover who or what yours is. Describe this oppressive force and decide if you need to continue being a victim.

Discovery is the key.

Succulent Second Month

The Land of No

week one

A Game or Something to Try

Smash Something INANIMATE

Old dishes, gifts you don't like. My friend Val throws overripe tomatoes at the wall. You can create a small ritual and let the smashing release a part of yourself that is stuck, crabby or in need of expansion.

Write a Rejection Letter

Write to the parts of yourself or people who stop you or inhibit your creative dreams. You don't need to mail it for it to be effective. "Dear _____, I have received your feedback and have decided that it doesn't apply to me, my life, or my creative dreams. Please consult the guidelines for reapplication before communicating again. Thank you and good-bye."

A GIFT for You

I SEND YOU . . .

A cottage retreat on a hill in Ireland. This cottage is filled with fresh flowers, art supplies, and a double-wide chaise lounge in front of a wood-burning fireplace. There is a cabinet near the front door, where your favorite meals appear, several times a day. Desserts are plentiful and calorie-free. The closet is stocked with colorful robes and pajamas, and a painting in the bedroom slides aside to reveal a plasma television screen with every movie you've ever wanted to watch. A wooden mailbox at the end of the lane is filled daily with beguiling invitations to tea parties, horse-and-carriage rides, theatrical performances, and violin concerts. There is no obligation or need to respond.

You sleep deeply and peacefully each night, and feel profoundly healthy. This cottage is yours to return to at any time.

i
send
you
deep
peace

"All Life is an experiment" ralph waldo emerson

week three

A Positive Challenge (I Dare You)

Transform Your Fears

TAKE YOUR MAIN FEAR about living more of your creative dreams and describe it in detail. For example:

"I won't have enough money to live on." Expand that thought until you end up with the worst thing that can happen (I'll starve and lose my apartment) and ask the strongest, sturdiest part of yourself to answer that fear with practical, realistic reassurances:

"I can always get a job."

"I will never starve."

"There will always be somewhere to live."

"I am capable and full of choices."

"I could always stay at _____ house."

week four

RADIANT Resources

Love Is Letting Go of Fear
Gerald A. Jampolsky, M.D.

Don't Push the River
Barry Stevens

Procrastination: Why You Do It, What To Do About It
Jane B. Burica and Lenora M. Yuen

Never Good Enough: How to Use Perfectionism to Your Advantage without Letting It Ruin Your Life
Monica Basco

Embracing Your Inner Critic: Turning Self-Criticism into a Creative Asset
Hal Stone, Ph.D. and Sidra Stone, Ph.D.

Inner Bonding: Becoming a Loving Adult to Your Inner Child
Margaret Paul, Ph.D.

Forgive for Good: A Proven Prescription for Health and Happiness
Dr. Fred Luskin

Let It Go: Burn, Bury, Rip, Repeat: And Make Way for What Makes You Healthier, Happier, Wealthier, Wiser
Joanna Arettam

www.lifechallenges.org
www.forthelittleonesinside.com
www.helpyourselftherapy.com
www.learningtoforgive.com
www.voicedialogue.com
www.spiritualityhealth.com

CHAPTER THREE

Treasured
Third Month

The World of Yes

The purpose of this chapter is to identify all the reasons you can and will live your creative dreams. It answers the question, "What starts you?"

Love

IMAGINE A WORLD where love is everywhere, where yes is the conscious answer. That world exists inside us now. It is our love for ourselves and the world that leads us to have creative dreams. Love can be strengthened, leaned on, employed, and deployed. Love is the sturdy initiator. Our creative dreams are fueled and fanned by love.

fan of love

IT IS OUR SELF-LOVE that leads us to make our creative dreams real. Loving the self requires practice. It is much more difficult to love ourselves than to criticize and experience self-hatred and doubt.

When we are out of love for and with ourselves, our creative dreams will falter.

Love is still the answer.

Self-love skillfully applied can create miracles. Each self-loving person living his or her creative dreams is an enormous power and force in our world. It is a natural source of power and energy.

Letting Declaring
Our Real
Visions Energetic
Emerge Aims
 More

Love is the most visible in the world of YES.
The word YES has an intrinsic power. Yes is an affirmation, an invitation, an answer of positive energy.

Our creative dreams need many yeses (and consciously applied nos). We visualize our creative dreams and some part of us says YES.

I can do that . . .

It can happen . . .

We can build it . . .

We will magnetize, manifest, make it

YES IS A MOTIVATOR. Yes is a crowd-pleaser, a barn raiser, a sign of plenty. Yes is in evidence when there is no evidence. We can choose to make our creative dream real in a world of yes.

With the full support of love and yes, new inventions can be born, raised, and work for our world. I think of two love-based YES organizations:

Paul Newman (Newman's Own)

Habitat for Humanity

And there are so many others

What will **love** and **yes** do for your creative dreams? How will your creative dreams grow in their light and care?

Willingness

WILLINGNESS HAS THE LETTERS of yes in it except for the Y. The Y stands for YOU which is the essence of willingness.

WILLINGNESS IS THE ABILITY TO MOVE WITHOUT PROOF. When we are willing, we are open and available for whatever is needed.

Willingness swirls all around our creative dreams. The question is built in: What are you willing to do for your creative dreams?

Willingness doesn't care if we are crabby, tired, or uninspired. Willingness is the cupcake maker for yet another fund-raiser.

CUPCAKES
Are
Quite DARLING

Willingness is like a secret ingredient. We can have money, business plans, and investors for our creative dreams, yet without willingness, it's a bit flat or stale.

Our willingness to learn, grow, apply ourselves, ask for help, respond to requests, and make ourselves available, can be practiced and made stronger.

Our willingness has sheer power and force to make changes.

Willingness = change

Our creative dreams thrive on applied willingness

We can ask ourselves over and over: Am I willing to be of service to my creative dreams?

We can also ask:

What am I not willing to do?

Willingness is our choice, and can be chosen with love in mind.

If we are unwilling and force it, we are not applying love.

We can explore willingness without automatically responding with a yes.

Carefully chosen YESes and NOs are basic to building our creative dreams.

Practice telling the truth faster to yourself and others, using your solar plexus as a guide. When we are willing and it's natural, the answer will naturally come from that center in our body. If we only use our mind, we can be misled.

Willingness can be measured in increments less than full-strength. We may be willing to make phone calls for our creative dreams, but not show up in person.

What are you really willing to do or be for your creative dreams?

Self-Acceptance
(Radical Variety)

IN ORDER TO LIVE OUR CREATIVE DREAMS, we need to accept ourselves as we actually are (not as we idealize we are).

SELF-ACCEPTANCE IS MORE CHALLENGING when we realize that it means accepting what we hate or find repulsive about ourselves, or just find less than.

Whatever we don't accept about ourselves will find its way into our creative dream life. Lack of self-acceptance leads to lack of deserving, which leads to creative dreams not becoming real.

If we don't accept ourselves, we won't accept all or part of our creative dreams. We can practice self-acceptance and still wish to change or improve parts of ourselves. The basis of radical self-acceptance asks us to accept how or who we already are before we make any changes or improvements.

In the beginning stages, our creative dreams can be fragile and vulnerable to attack. Any lack of self-acceptance accelerates any weakness in our creative dreams.

Self-acceptance is a foundation aspect of creative dream-living and dream-making. When our foundations are strongly and solidly in place, creative dream-making can much more easily take shape and flight. You can increase your solid foundation by stating and learning to believe the following:

yes yes yes yes yes yes yes yes

"I accept my procrastination, and intend to learn new ways to work with it."

If we are out of acceptance with our procrastination, it will ruin us and our creative dreams.

"I dream of doing that, but I've always been a procrastinator . . ." Sigh . . .

The unspoken message is that we're helpless somehow with procrastination. By naming that we practice procrastination, we may think we've accepted it. But usually we're only resigned to it.

Acceptance leads to expansive change.

When and what we accept, we can change.

Self-acceptance is a benefit like awareness.

Often awareness is all that's needed for a shift to take place.

You can increase your experiences of radical self-acceptance by:

Identifying areas where you lack self-acceptance. This awakens you further for possible change.

Being willing to allow these places in you to exist. This allowing causes more movement than resisting or denying.

Sharing your experiences about self-acceptance with others.

This reminds you that you are not the only one, and gives you support.

Energy

Energy IS OUR CREATIVE DREAM-MAKING POWER SOURCE. It is a completely free, clean, renewable source of power that can be studied, practiced, and enhanced.

We measure energy by how we feel in our minds, bodies and spirits.

Our creative dreams are run by and on our energy.

If energy is low, we feel depleted, deflated, and our creative dreams will receive very little nourishment.

If energy is high, we feel refreshed, inspired, and energized, and our creative dreams will be fed and expanded upon.

We can learn to run our energy on consistent, drama-free platforms.

Our energy builds and grows with our care and attention.

What makes our energy expand:

Oxygen

Sunlight

Water

Love

Support

Visioning/visualizing

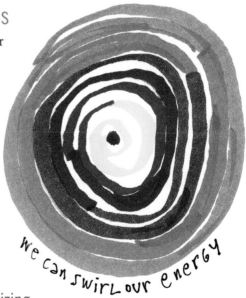

we can swirl our energy

What makes our energy contract?

Toxins
Lack of love
Codependence
Isolation
Stress
Worry

We can promote our energy with enthusiasm and focus in the following ways:

Study and practice new ways of energy expansion

You can do this by learning what gives you energy and choosing to do those things more often. If you're stuck with your creative dream, choose an activity that delights or inspires you.

Gather energetic community

You can do this by learning what kinds of people energize you, and spend more time with them. Energizing people are interesting and expansive, and cause creative movement.

Engage in activities that cause energy gains

You can do this by studying your patterns of activity and choosing ones that replenish your energy. Make a list of activities that most often refresh you. Keep this list nearby.

What is your "energy style"? Are you:

Fast moving

You can arrange your life and work to coincide with your energy style. This will give you more energy for creative dream-living.

Slow and deliberate

Move energetically at your pace, even if it's at a different speed. Your natural energetic style will serve your creative dream life.

Medium with highs and lows

You can provide experiences that satisfy your various speeds and energy style. This will allow energy to flow consistently.

Are you able to determine how you best operate energetically?

You can do this by exploring what drains you and what refills you, and how often you experience each of these states.

Can you spend more time learning about being energetically refreshed?

You can do this by studying energy as a subject, and how energy moves in your particular spirit.

You can explore and experiment with energy and use it to activate your creative dreams.

Inner Allies, Teachers, and Mentors

Inner Allies

Our inside critics are actually allies gone awry. We can empower ourselves as allies for our creative dreams.

Each critical voice you hear is trying to protect you from something.

> Better not try to dream—you'll end up in the poorhouse.
>
> Don't leave your job before you've lined up another; you remember what happened last time.
>
> Dreamers never really get anywhere.
>
> How much more time are you going to waste on that dream?

The inside critics are preoccupied with loss. The inner allies are helpers involved with gain.

"If you try that dream, you might really increase your cash flow."

"You could take a leap of faith and just leave that job."

"Dreamers are full of energy and resources."

"Look at how far you've gotten with your dream already!"

We are our own best champions and inner allies of our creative dreams.

Ally means: To unite or combine; helper.

We can expand our capabilities with inner allies by calling them into being and focus. We can describe ourselves this way, "I'll get my inner allies to work on it."

Your inner allies are your "glow team." They're the ones who say yes to you and your creative dreams. These allies can be actual people in your life, people you admire, or imaginary characters you invent.

You can assemble your inner allies in a journal, or make a poster of their photographs. You can bring them to life by drawing, writing about, painting, or sculpting them.

You can ask your inner allies questions about your creative dreams. Sometimes I write a note or letter to my inner allies, and leave it for a period of time. Often when I return, the answer appears.

Inner allies are always on your side. They offer acknowledgment, support, validation, courage, praise and love.

Teachers and Mentors

We can be self-taught and taught by others. Teachers can appear in books, films, or by our experiences.

Being teachable is a subject for study and practice. We can need or want to learn, yet be essentially unteachable. If we are stubborn, or unwilling to listen or change, we can be unteachable. (I was like this for a long time.)

Our creative dreams often need teaching of various descriptions:

Obtaining skills

 Obtaining information

Surrender to the teachings

If we are rebellious, we will often seek teachers on our own terms, in books or at workshops.

However we receive teachings, our creative dreams will benefit from learning.

We can learn any number of things and only use some of it.

Our teaching/learning methods can be experimented with all of our lives, with all of our creative dreams.

A mentor is already doing/living something you want to do or live.

You can apply to this person for mentoring. It is usually free.

The mentoring process is a practical, alchemical process. Practical, because you can imitate or practice what he or she has done and apply it to your own life. Alchemical, because his or her energy and your energy merge and change both of you.

Mentors can mentor very briefly or over a lifetime. Coaching is a form of paid mentoring and is very effective for creating movement and change.

Most people have been mentored in their lives, which usually leads them to mentor. It is a circular gift that continues giving through generations.

Some of my mentors are or have been:

Henry Miller (taught me about living my creative dreams)

Maya Angelou (taught me to develop my courage)

Cheri Huber (role model for meditating no matter what you're resisting)

Patricia Huntington (personal and business coaching)

Miriam Wornum (crone wisdom)

Rebecca Latimer (profound lessons about death and living a creative life)

Isabel Collins (role model for living succulently with class and elegance)

iSABeL WAS
LiKe A WiLD
MUSiC iN MY
Life . . .

Who are your mentors? Can you list and describe them? If you don't currently have any, can you describe qualities or teachings they might offer you?

Building Your Dream Life

"If you build it, it might fall down."—SARK

Building your "dream life" is filled with things that can feel like the opposite of a dream:

☆ Mistakes

Delays

Starting over ☆

Failure

THE BUILDING PART is actually more of a rebuilding that is a continual process. The building is not linear in nature, but far more interesting. You might start a creative dream, take the "next step," and find yourself completely bored, dissatisfied, or just not inspired. These experiences might lead you to try something completely different, or just do part of what you started.

As you build, you might encounter brand-new experiences that thrill you or motivate you. This might lead you to rebuild your creative dream in a whole new way.

Creative dream-building involves change, and fear of change.

Remember that in the world of Yes, Fear = Contraction. When we contract, we become closed or restricted. This can cause us to retreat or give up.

Take a look at what causes you to contract or expand with regard to your creative dreams.

Creative dreams themselves are natural expansion devices. They contain energy, motion, and desire.

WE CAN LEARN TO RESPOND to change creatively by studying our habitual responses and making adjustments. It can feel natural to respond to change by contracting or saying no.

Contraction is not bad, it just slows expansion.

What makes you feel expansive, open to change, and like saying Yes?

I think that we need an internal sense of safety and knowledge of ourselves in order to be expansive with our creative dreams.

We can build this sense of safety and knowledge by study and practice.

In my creative dream-building process, I am consistently challenging my responses to change.

INITIALLY, I FEEL EXPANSIVE when I try something new, and then contract as soon as I encounter difficulty or the unknown. I am learning to experiment with my tolerance of difficulty and the not knowing, in order to go further with my creative dreams. It is always a combination of contraction and expansion.

As I build and rebuild my creative dream life, I am always asking,

"What would it take for me to expand on this?"

Whenever I experience contraction, I explore it by asking,
"Where did I stop and why?"

Sometimes the building takes the shape of tearing down and stripping away of what is not real and true.

Building a creative dream life is not just about achieving, succeeding, or "meeting goals." It is also about floundering, stumbling, tripping, and failing.

Build a way to weave them together, and your success will be measured by the process of your creative dream life, and not the progress.

The Courage to
LET LOOSE the Wonders Inside You

WE ARE ALL FILLED WITH WONDERS. Somewhere inside, you know this, even if you haven't made it real yet.

The knowledge can give you courage to let these wonders be seen.

What else gives you courage?

I think that courage is activated by:

Evidence
Something that we tried that worked and we can see it

But what gives us the courage to try it in the first place?

I am often asked how I got the courage to go from being a "starving artist" to being a "successful artist."

I'm convinced that this courage was already inside me, and it got activated by things that I tried with absolutely no courage to start with.

I didn't try new things with courage and confidence, but rather with will and determination. The courage grew as I saw the evidence.

Yes

The will and determination that I exhibited grew out of my continuing to say Yes to my original creative dream of inspiring people.

I felt determined to say Yes because I had spent so many years saying No, and all those habitual unconscious Nos hadn't gotten me very far with creative dreams.

If I'd waited for courage to just appear, I think I'd still be starving. My courage was activated and strengthened by all of my consciously applied Yeses to my creative dreams.

When I began to let loose the wonders inside, I felt thrilled at what was in there.

It was so much more about my not letting it out than I ever realized.

Most of us have some version of an inside critic that says,

How dare you?

How **dare** you be creatively fulfilled and successful?

Because you have wonders inside that must be let loose, that is how you dare.

Let your daring dance with your wonders.

> From now on I hope always to stay alert, to educate myself as best I can. But lacking this, in Future I will relaxedly turn back to my secret mind to see what it has observed when I thought I was sitting this one out. We never sit anything out.
>
> We are cups, constantly and quietly being filled. The trick is, knowing how to tip ourselves over and let the beautiful stuff out.—RAY BRADBURY

While completing this book, I went for my evening walk and met a 70-year-old painter named Roy. We began discussing creative dreams and he said, "I hope you tell them it's all about letting loose the wonders inside." I explained excitedly that I had just written this section with that title!

Once again, I am reminded how creatively connected we all are.

WHAT if we All WALKed Around letting loose THe wonders inside of us?

Treasured Third Month

The World of Yes

week one

A Game or Something to Try

Create a Creative Dream-Making Map or Collage

FOR A WALL IN YOUR HOME. Sometimes when we keep things inside books, they can't get enough oxygen to take flight. Put up a big piece of white paper and glue things onto it that represent your creative dream. This will be a visual reminder of your creative dream and a powerful way to describe what is important to you with regard to your dream.

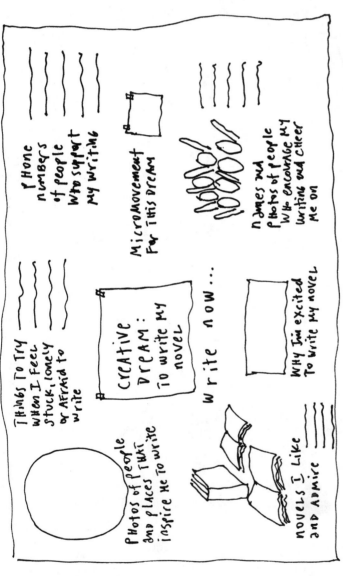

You'll need:

glue,

scissors,

tape,

old magazines,

duplicate

photographs,

markers,

big white paper.

PHOTOS of people and places that inspire me to write

Things to try when I feel stuck, lonely or afraid to write

Phone numbers of people who support my writing

CREATIVE DREAM: To write my novel

Micromovement for this dream

Write now...

novels I like and admire

Why I'm excited to write my novel

Names and photos of people who encourage my writing and cheer me on

Making a collage or map is a good way to keep your creative dream visible. This will also help you set your intention to make your dream real. You can also make a page like this for your guidebook if you rather work with a smaller size. Experiment with words and images and see what delights you.

A G I F T for You

I SEND YOU . . .

The gift of a letter from your wise self. This is the part of you that sees you with benevolent, loving eyes. You find this letter in a thick envelope with your name on it, and the word Yes written boldly above your name.

"My Dear,

I am writing this to remind you of your 'essence beauty.' This is the part of you that has nothing to do with age, occupation, weight, history, or pain. This is the soft, untouched, indelible you. You can love yourself in this moment, no matter what you have, or haven't done or been.

See past any masks, devices, or inventions that obscure your essence.

Remember your true purpose, WHICH is only Love.

If you cannot see or feel love, lie down now and cry; it will cleanse your vision and free your heart.

I love you, I am you."

week three

A Positive Challenge (I Dare You)

Visit Three New Websights

Use my resource list or someone else's.
Do three things about each websight:

"everything you can imagine is real" pablo picasso

1. Send an e-mail message of support to the creator.

2. List one creative dream support idea in your creative dream guidebook that you got from looking at the websight or just make a note of it.

3. Describe how you were affected.

Or, write to three people you admire and mail the letters.

Contacting people in this way creates an energetic circle that has a positive effect whether you receive a response or not.

☆
week four

RADIANT Resources

How to Think Like Leonardo Da Vinci
   Michael J. Gelb

Eat Mangoes Naked: Finding Pleasure Everywhere and Dancing with the Pits
   SARK

Creative Visualization: Use the Power of Your Imagination to Create What You Want in Your Life
   Shakti Gawain

Stand Still Like the Hummingbird
   Henry Miller

Imagine a Woman in Love With Herself: Embracing Your Wisdom and Wholeness
   Patricia Lynn Reilly

A Thousand Days in Venice: An Unexpected Romance
  Marlena deBlasi

Succulent Wild Woman: Dancing with Your Wonder-full Self
  SARK

www.sabrinawardharrison.com

www.freewillastrology.com

www.feistyscribe.com

www.marthabeck.com

CHAPTER FOUR

Feisty
Fourth Month

Making Creative Dreams Real with MicroMOVEments

The purpose of this chapter is to learn and practice the micromovement method, which works even if you don't want to.

What Are MicroMOVEments?

CREATIVE DREAMS CAN GET STUCK inside our heads, in drawers, inside computers, and in closets.

What gets them moving?

AS CREATIVE DREAMERS, we are all filled with fabulous ideas and descriptions relating to our creative dreams. We are also aware that some of what leads to a dream fulfilled may be tedious, mundane, boring, or just really time-consuming. If you are a practicing procrastinator, perfectionist, avoider, just plain busy, or want to stay in bed and not really do anything, micromovements are designed especially for you.

Do you have a short attention span?

Many of us do. I invented micromovements because of my short attention span. I procrastinated for years about all of my creative dreams.

I WOULD EMBARK ON A NEW PROJECT, filled with excitement and enthusiasm, and then would get distracted, lose interest, or just feel overwhelmed.

Every time I tried to follow through on exercises, plans, or goals, I would quit in the middle and feel like a pathetic failure.

Then I realized that I didn't have to complete a project all at once. I saw that I could

work in smaller bursts of energy and in much shorter increments of time. I could do just about anything for 5 minutes.

So I began experimenting with my new system and was astonished to discover how many things I was able to finish and complete.

A MICROMOVEMENT IS A VERY TINY ACTION that anyone can take toward some part of his or her creative dream. It's 5 seconds to 5 minutes in length, and you write it down, along with a gentle date and time for completion. I say gentle, because you can change it as many times as you need to.

A micromovement is 5 seconds to 5 minutes long because we can do just about anything for 5 seconds to 5 minutes.

You may begin and complete your micromovement and suddenly feel energized to continue on. That's great! Go galloping off for hours, days, or weeks of sheer activity.

Or simply complete your micromovement and go take a nap.

Or gently reschedule your next micromovement.

"How lovely to think that no one need wait a moment, we can start now, start slowly changing the world." Anne Frank

89

The reason it's a gentle date and time written down, is that most of us are too harsh and very self-critical.

Gentleness is a reminder that we can reschedule it as needed. The reason we write it down is to get it out of our heads.

Use Post-its or scraps of paper or napkins, matchbooks, or index cards.

Scrawl illegibly, print meticulously. Just write it down. This gets it out of your head and makes it separate from you.

Then it can be an action and not a rehearsal inside your head.

Micromovements are powerfull helpers for our creative dreams because they create a habit of completion. Most procrastinators excel in not completing things. Completing your micromovement will give you a new attitude about your creative dreams.

You can be very busy and still find 5 minutes or less for a micromovement. It will substantially reinforce your feelings of success and progress.

You can also accelerate your creative dreams by practicing multiple micromovements.

☆

Examples of MicroMOVEments

OUR CREATIVE DREAMS NEED SUPPORT SERVICES. These include phone calls, letters, and other tasks that may seem mundane.

Much of what stops us is the ordinary.

We think of our creative dream and imagine what needs to happen before it can become true and real, and we sigh and stop ourselves.

Here's a classic list of what we don't want to, or just don't do, with regard to our creative dreams:

Balance checkbooks

Call for help

Apply for a loan

Write a grant

Organize photos

Buy art supplies

Research

Clean our closets

Remember: Procrastinators are fabulous rehearsers. They mentally rehearse endlessly without physically moving.

Micromovements are a cure for inertia

You could ask a procrastinator to paint the bedroom, and she might lie on the couch mentally preparing to paint, rehearsing what kind of brushes she will use, and what color paint to buy. When you ask her when she'll be starting, she might say, **"I'll do it later, I'm too tired now."** And she never actually made any physical movement!

Stories of Success and Stumbling

My mother asked me to share her story of micromovements.

At 79 years old, she had a risky surgery to repair a replaced hip. She experienced medication-induced delusions that resulted in her mysterious fall at the nursing home after her surgery. The fall caused the bone that had just been repaired 2 weeks before to shatter into hundreds of pieces.

A new surgery repaired that bone. She was then told she would never walk again and never leave the nursing home.

With the help of an incredible team of physical therapists, healers, and loving care, and thousands of micromovements, my mother left the nursing home and is walking again.

She holds up one arm and says resolutely, **"You tell them I practiced my micromovements."**

WHEN WE ARE YOUNG, MICROMOVEMENTS ARE THE WAY WE MOVE! THIS IS MY MOM AT AGE 1

A woman in her 60s wrote to me and said this:

"My husband died and he was a watch repair person. He had his shop in our backyard, and I'd like to do something with it. My creative dream is to paint. Can you help with micromovements?"

Her first micromovement was to open the door to the watch repair studio. That was the most difficult one, because of all the memories in that studio. After she completed that micromovement, she stopped for a few months. When she resumed her micromovement practice, she was ready for change.

Hundreds of micromovements later, the studio was empty except for an easel and art supplies sitting on the hardwood floor.

After more micromovements, she began painting, and not long after she began exhibiting her work in local galleries.

A woman wrote to me and said, *"I've tried your micromovement method and it isn't working for me. Any suggestions?"*

Her creative dream was to open a health food store. I asked if she would share her micromovement and she supplied it:

Rent a store and order inventory to fill it

She explained that that was her first micromovement and she hadn't been able to complete it. I gently asked her if it was 5 seconds to 5 minutes in length, or if there was a date and time, and she said, *"No, but I don't have the time to do it so slowly."*

I asked her if she has the time to never do it.

There was a great silence. She laughed and said, *"O.K. Help me understand the micromovement method."*

We assembled a new plan, and her first micromovements were:

1. Call her cousin George in the commercial real estate business Friday by 2 P.M.

2. Make a lunch date with George Thursday at 2 P.M.

3. Reschedule lunch with George for Monday at 1 P.M.

4. Call bank manager at 10 A.M. Tuesday for loan application.

It went on from there, until she located a storefront, obtained a loan, took a small business education class at community college, and traveled to another state to visit her friend who owns a health food store.

As it turned out, her creative dream shifted as she uncovered more information and she decided not to open a health food store. She was eagerly choosing her next creative dream and micromovement the last time I heard from her.

Micromovements continue to support my creative dreams. I often have dozens of Post-its on my wall with micromovements written down. Of course, because I teach and speak about this system, my friends will often ask, "Have you chosen a micromovement?" if I get stuck or scared, which is often.

I have learned that it uses more energy to resist or avoid taking action than it does to make a micromovement.

Every creative dream I've made real exists because of hundreds or thousands of micromovements.

I'm inspired when I hear from parents using micromovements with their kids. One mother wrote and told me that her 8-year-old son uses micromovements for his homework and to get ready for school in the mornings, and that their household routines have really benefited and changed as a result.

I'm very inspired by Christopher Reeve, who practices micromovements with his body.

Practice and Process with MicroMOVEments

CREATIVE DREAM

To travel to Europe and paint

MICROMOVEMENT: Saturday at 10 A.M.
Take my passport application out of the drawer and fondle it lovingly

CREATIVE DREAM

To write a novel

MICROMOVEMENT: Sunday at 2 P.M.
Turn on my computer and open file called "Novel"

CREATIVE DREAM

To go on a satisfying romantic date with a man

MICROMOVEMENT: Friday at 7 P.M.
Call Larry about 8-minute dating and ask his experience

After you've completed one micromovement, it's time to choose another. Here are some next micromovements for the three creative dreams.

CREATIVE DREAM

To travel to Europe and paint

MICROMOVEMENT: Call Val at 3 P.M. on Sunday about her friend living in Italy painting

CREATIVE DREAM

To write a novel

MICROMOVEMENT: Friday at 7 P.M. go to bookstore and browse books about writing

CREATIVE DREAM

To go on a date

MICROMOVEMENT: Go to websight www.8minutedating.com at 5 P.M. Saturday and see when the next event is in my age group

What is one of your creative dreams? ☆

Choose a micromovement and write it here

Is it 5 seconds to 5 minutes in length? Does it have a gentle date and time written down?
If you're ready, choose another.

Micromovements rapidly become easier and easier the more you practice them.

A micromovement is like a light switch, an ignition system, an inspirational device.

Some people will be able to use micromovements instantly, choosing one after another. Others will move more deliberately, choosing one and waiting a long time to choose the next.

This is fine! There is no scale of progress for micromovements that says more is better. This is a system for you, to work in your life, on your creative dreams, not someone else's.

Even if you're not ready to practice with micromovements, it is still valuable for you to read this and know they're there if you need them.

MicroMOVEment Wheel

A MICROMOVEMENT WHEEL is a good way to keep moving if you're ready for more activity with your creative dream. (If you're not ready, just reading and seeing this will affect you positively.)

MicroMOVEment Buddies

MANY OF US have our creative dreams alone, or feel isolated with them.

With whom and how do you share your creative dreams?

Sharing micromovements is an excellent way to keep or get creative dreams moving. Having a friendly witness is a boon for the spirit and a creative dream accelerator.

You can share micromovements by phone, e-mail, or letter, or in person at a café.

Find a friend that you will feel safe and comfortable with and one who wants to also practice micromovements.

You can choose a micromovement about establishing a micromovement buddy system!

E-mail is a great way to practice micromovements. You can send your micromovement to your micromovement buddy and then check in about your experience.

MicroMOVement WHeeL

THis is A Good WAY To keep Moving if you're reADY For More Activity WiTH your creAtive DreAM. (if you're noT reADY, JVST reADing and seeing THis will Affect you positively)

PvT A creAtive DREAM into THe Middle circle and CHOOse MicroMovements THAT correspond.

reminDer: MicroMOVements Are 5 seconds – 5 Minutes in lenGTH

10. SunDAY 3pm Practice knitting WHile WATCHing T.V.

11. TvesDAY 4pm TAKe Knitting to TanyA's House and TAlk ABout it

FriDAY 6pm knit First row of sleeve of sweAter

12.

1. SATurDAY 4pm CAll VALerie for pAtterns or online resources

9. FriDAY 6pm Attend First knitting clAss

CreAtive DreAM: To knit A sweAter

2. WeDnesDAY 11 AM Cut out pictures of sweAters I Like in MAgAzines

8. weDnesDAY 7pm Go to VALerie's House For Dinner and see WHAT SHe's knitting

7. SunDAY 3pm Visit knitting store and look AT and look AT supplies

FriDAY 1pm register By pHone For knitting clAss

TvesDAY 4pm CAll THe ART SCHOOL For referrals For knitting clAsses

SunDAY 1pm DrAw A sketch of My DreAM sweAter

FriDAY 3pm visit store in My neighborhood THAT HAs Hand knit Things

3.

6.

5.

4.

Here are common experiences:

Oh, I forgot to do my micromovement!

I got too scared

I realized it was the wrong micromovement

I can't seem to pick just one

Wow! I did it!

Can you help me choose the next one?

I rescheduled it

I rescheduled it again

I decided to pick a new one

Be sure you have an agreement about gentleness and nonjudgment.

Micromovements are not for challenging or judging.

Just keep checking in about your micromovement experience.

Make a decision not to compare your micromovement experience with your friend. It's tempting to do that, especially if your friend is speeding along with his or her micromovement and you're not.

Micromovements come in all shapes and speeds. There is no comparison.

Some creative dreams call for more difficult micromovements, and people are ready to move at different times. There are many reasons why we move at the speeds we do.

More micromovements doesn't mean it's better!

Ask for help if you see your micromovement buddy having an easier time. See if you feel like discussing what frightens you or feels different.

You can use this book to do micromovements week by week or month by month, or go to my websight for free, downloadable micromovement worksheets: www.campsark.com.

You can also have more than one micromovement buddy for different creative dreams. Sometimes one person is a better fit for a particular creative dream.

You can also ask someone to be your micromovement buddy even if she's not working with micromovements or on creative dreams.

She is just a witness to your micromovement process. Ask her to be a gentle, nonjudging friend for your experiment. If she seems unwilling or confused, ask someone else.

MICROMOVEMENTS changed my creative life and dreams. I am now able to complete most things. I always have a place to start from, which is essential for making creative dreams real.

"Making it real" requires consistent actions and developing dreams into something that you and others can see, feel, or experience.

The creative dreams I have made real can now travel without me. When creative dreams are only in our minds, we must be present to describe and explain them. This limits their life span.

Use micromovements to give your creative dreams

Great

Big

Flapping

Wings!

Feisty Fourth Month

Making Creative Dreams Real with MicroMOVEments

week one

A Game or Something to Try

Have a Creative Dream Time with Yourself

TAKE YOURSELF OUT for an adventure. Bring along your creative dream guidebook or a notebook, and an exploratory mood. (You can go without this mood—it may develop along the way.) Be prepared to eat by yourself, go to a film, or walk in nature somewhere.

Solo adventures can awaken new dreams.

Succulent

Open

Luscious

Options

See what develops and take notes if you wish. This has the potential to nurture and encourage you to become intimate with your solitude, which is one of your strongest creative dream development centers.

week two

A G I F T for You

I SEND YOU . . .

Deep summer and a glistening bowl of raspberries. You lie in bed on a screened-in porch and wonder whether a thunderstorm is coming. The window screen is warm on your fingertips and a tiny breeze is beginning. You smile slightly and reach for the cotton sheet to prepare for the rain and wind to start. You put a raspberry on each fingertip and eat them all that way. Your Life is Juicy, no matter what comes your way.

☆

week three

A Positive Challenge (I Dare You)

Send me your creative dream(s): www.planetsark.com.
I am collecting creative dreams as a kind of giant "dream-catcher." Posting your creative dream will give it power and energy, and is part of "making it real." Join our marvelous community of creative dream livers.

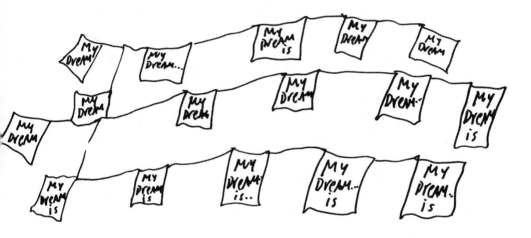

i see it AS A PArADe of
prAyer FlAGs

SHAre your creAtive DreAM WiTH Me

RADIANT Resources

The Artist's Way: A Spiritual Path to Higher Creativity
Julia Cameron

The Bodacious Book of Succulence:
Daring to Live Your Succulent Wild Life
SARK

Your Handwriting Can Change Your Life
Vimala Rodgers

Peace Pilgrim: Her Life and Work in Her Own Words
Peace Pilgrim

A String and a Prayer: How to Make and Use Prayer Beads
Eleanor Wiley and Maggie Oman Shannon

Nothing Is Impossible: Reflections on a New Life
Christopher Reeve

Intimacy and Solitude: Balancing Closeness and Independence
Stephanie Dowrick

I Could Do Anything If Only I Knew What It Was
Barbara Sher

www.thenewstory.com
www.spiralmuse.com
www.barbarasher.com
www.center-for.com

CHAPTER FIVE

Fabulous
Fifth Month

Creative Dreams
Support Systems

The purpose of this chapter is to assist you in building or adding to your support system, and reminding you that you are not alone.

How Can Your Friends and Family Support Your Creative Dreams?

MANY CREATIVE DREAMS are hidden or not discussed with family and friends.

Often friends and family focus on "what's happening" instead of a more interior process.

The shaping and evolving of a creative dream usually takes time, practice, patience, and assistance.

You can ask your friends and family for help with all of these.

Show them this book and explain you'll be working with it to help make your creative dreams real

Then ask for their help. Let them know what your creative dream is.

Ask them to support you by asking only positive questions. Explain that you are being challenged by yourself and by the book, and that you want family and friends to be a "resting place" free of criticism and challenge.

If you can work differently with a friend or family member, describe and explain what you're learning and how he or she can assist.

Usually friends and family just want your creative dream to be real and you to be happy.

You can ask for their patience with the parts where you stumble, get lost, want to give up, or start all over with a different creative dream.

Ask them not to judge your seeking a life made of creative dreams.

Ask them to celebrate your tiny movements as well as the larger ones.

Ask them about their creative dreams and see if you can open a dialogue about this.

Many of us never know or knew our parents' creative dreams. Asking them can be enormously interesting.

Some of us have best friends without knowing their creative dreams.

When we have children our creative dreams often get so postponed or put away that it takes some investigating to uncover them.

If you have something from your creative dream to share or show family or friends, let them know what you want. Usually we only want encouragement and support. Especially at the egg phase.

Later in the creative dream phase, we can ask for "constructive criticism."

Let's define that:

Who is criticizing? Do you trust and respect that person?

Can she deliver constructive criticism in positive language?

What is she being constructive about? Is it a blend or a balance of both?

Is she trying to be right? Is she trying to protect you?

Does she do her own work with creative dreams?

Proceed slowly and cautiously with constructive criticism. Often people have heard things that stop their creative dream progress for a very long time.

You can assist people by telling them exactly how they can best provide feedback.

"I know that this part is vague. Do you have suggestions about how I can make it more specific?"

"I know that my plan leaves out the whole financial aspect. Do you have any ideas about how I can best change that?"

"When I move to performance, I will value your attendance. Can you imagine now what you'd like to see/experience in my show?"

Ask friends and family for specific kinds of support. Support them for their creative dreams.

"BUT THOU GODS DARLING! HEED THY PRIVATE DREAM"

RALPH WALDO EMERSON

Assist them in understanding what is supportive for you specifically.

Remember: friends and family will rely on what they know or have experienced with regard to understanding your creative dreams.

Do not take personally any of their fears, criticisms, judgments, or concerns.

Assist them in understanding you and your creative dreams.

Requests from and Invitations to People You Don't Know

YOUR CREATIVE DREAM may guide you to contact someone you don't know. This is good and we all practice it.

Here are some guidelines for best results:

No Expectations or Attachments

Send your requests or invitations without expecting a response. You can still expect something, just don't blame the person if you don't hear from him. We are all busy, involved people with various forms of administrative support. You may be contacting someone who is at capacity, or has no one dedicated to responding.

Be Brief, Specific, and Charming

It's best to abbreviate whatever you're asking so it can be read very quickly. Ask directly for what you want without a lot of explanation.

Say something that isn't usually said.

Inspire and Get the Person Involved

Let him know how he or his work has affected or influenced you.

Reference his work correctly.

Explain your request in a way that's engaging and has some details that are compelling.

Send him a quote that inspires you.

Again, be brief.

Make It Easy and Simple to Respond

Send an SASE (self-addressed, stamped envelope) so whatever you're sending can be returned at no expense.

Give your phone number, e-mail, and address at each juncture (so many people contact me and then say, "You'll probably never call so I won't leave my number." Now I can't call them!)

E-mail is very easy and simple.

Practice Gratitude

Send a thank-you, even if he didn't help that much or give you what you dreamed of!

Creative Dream Teams

IF YOU'VE WORKED ALONE with your creative dream and would appreciate having support from other people, you might consider joining or forming a team. This team can consist of two or more members, and can be specifically chosen or designed to fit your particular personality and creative dreams.

Some suggestions for forming a team:

(You can also use these suggestions for joining a team)

Ask yourself the following questions:

Would I benefit most from joining or forming a team?

What size team would I most enjoy?

Where would I meet this team?

Short-term, long-term, or open-ended?

What would I want to receive from this team?

What would I want to offer?

How much time do I want to spend?

How often would we meet?

What structure would best suit me?

Your answers will provide good information about your actual interest in being part of a team. If you'd like to form a team, here are some additional thoughts and ideas:

Choose a pace for your team with regard to your creative dream development. You might want to ask for other people with a creative dream at a similar stage to yours, or you might want a mixture of people at different stages.

Establish safety and boundaries. Decide as a team if communications within the team are to be kept private or shared with other people. Discuss how or whether to keep criticism and judgment out of each other's creative dream and processes.

Decide on a timeline. Is your team going to communicate:

Daily	Quarterly
Weekly	Randomly
Monthly	Yearly

Choose whether your team will meet:

In person

Not in person

If in person, decide where you will meet

If not in person, decide which communication method works best

Choose how your team will function:

Decide how and when new people can join in, or if your team will consist of the original members.

Consider the structure of your time with the team:

How is time handled?

Is there a leader?

Do you wish to create team guidelines?

There are many ways to set up a structure for your team, or you might wish to be much more informal. Here are some additional ideas that will be especially useful for larger teams:

You might have as part of your team something called "introductions," where each new person introduces herself, her creative dream, and reason for wanting to be part of a team.

There could be a section called "celebrations and acknowledgments," where each team member's progress or experience with her creative dream is recognized.

You can discuss the subject of shadow material within your team. As a team works together, it is common for jealousies, projections, comparisons, judgments, blame, and competition to arise. You can decide whether to process this material individually or within the team. You can also choose to focus on positive, creative dream experiences only.

We have a lot more opportunities now for creating teams on the Internet. Teams can function really well by e-mail and there are many to choose from.

As an introvert, I'm especially grateful for the possibility of joining or forming a "virtual team." I know that we don't need to be alone with our creative dreams unless we choose to.

Providing Support for Yourself

MANY OF US ARE BETTER at providing support for others than we are at providing support for ourselves. We still think it's selfish to focus on ourselves, as though there's a finite supply of support.

If we do not learn to support ourselves, our creative dreams will not be able to grow and flourish. There will simply be no foundational basis.

Providing support for yourself involves a series of skills and practices that anyone can do. It is also an art that requires repetition and consciousness.

Let's define support:

It is a feeling of solidity, constancy, and an underlying ongoing base of help and assistance.

1. Do you deserve support? From yourself?

We might quickly answer "Yes!" then if we explore further, we might find that aspects of ourselves don't feel deserving of support.

"After all, I really didn't work all that hard."

"Other people are a lot worse off then me."

"Support is all relative I suppose."

"Who really feels supported in this life?"

2. Learn to feel deserving of support for yourself

Examine your belief systems about support. Learn about being self-supporting. Make changes if there are areas where you don't support yourself.

3. Define and describe your particular systems of support in the areas of:

PHYSICAL: nutrition, exercise, fresh air, sunshine, fun with your body, sexuality

What are you doing now to support your physical self?

EMOTIONAL: feeling, experiencing, psychological awareness

What are you doing now to support your emotional self?

MENTAL: learning, reading, new skills, listening, creating, studying

What are you doing now to support your mental self?

SPIRITUAL: prayer, meditation, seeking, ritual, nature, allowing

What are you doing now to support your spiritual self?

When we are self-supporting, we are better able to support our creative dreams. What our creative dreams need to grow may require strength that we wouldn't have without self-supporting skills.

We all have areas of self-support that are more developed than others. For example, I don't really cook very much, so my nutritional support needs to be monitored. Sometimes I tend to be isolated, so my social skills can be expanded.

Self-support is a highly sensitive operation.
If one area is out of balance, it can take the feeling of support away from other areas. Recently I was exercising a lot

more than I usually do, and found out that I wasn't supporting my quiet, reflective parts—in fact, I was running away from those parts.

Think of having a dial, or a scale on all your systems of self-support.

Stay focused on what feels supportive to you, even if it feels vulnerable or unfamiliar. Sometimes what supports us is the most difficult thing to find or obtain.

A sturdy platform is a fine thing to launch from

I like to speak about "sturdy platforms of support," and I encourage you to build one for yourself.

Then you can stand squarely on it and orchestrate your creative dreams.

The more you learn to provide support for yourself, the more that support will become obvious, like oxygen or sunlight.

Many of us learn just enough self-support to function. We can go far beyond this, and become experts in our own support systems.

Another creative dream support system is inspiration. When we feel inspired, we can do just about anything.

Who or What Inspires You?

YOUR CREATIVE DREAMS are nourished by inspiration. To inspire is to "give breath."

Your being inspired gives breath to your creative dreams.

What inspires you?

I believe that the daily and ordinary contain all the inspiration we need to grow huge creative dreams. Here are some experiences that have inspired me recently:

Glistening blueberries in a purple bowl

Moist soil around newly planted seeds

Slant of sunlight on the chaise longue

Angry child softening into laughter

Warm, wide paw of a dog in your hand

IN ORDER TO KNOW what inspires you, you must be able to see it. This requires what I call "special vision."

You can develop special vision for inspiration. It involves:

Looking closely

Moving more slowly

Letting love in

Being willing to be moved

Practicing this special vision involves:

Exploring your world in new ways

Allowing adventure

Abandoning your plans

Inventing new routes

Who inspires you?
Can you describe them, or make a list?
What qualities do inspiring people have?

Something uncommon or slightly askew

Surprise

Eccentricity

Ordinarily unusual

Ability to engage

Inspiring people are all around us, just waiting to be engaged.

My friend Tanya and I are very inspired by our friend Isabel, who recently celebrated her 90th birthday and shared the following:

Tanya asked her if it was difficult to accept all the changes in the area after so many years, and Isabel replied:

"Oh, all the changes have been for the better."

We were both inspired by this viewpoint about change, and by Isabel's fierce positive energy and enthusiasm.

Uncovering and finding inspiring people involves:

Asking (who are they?)

Listening (to what they say)

Becoming involved (what are they doing?)

Extending yourself (how can you become involved?)

I FELT VERY INSPIRED by the author May Sarton, and eagerly read all her books. She was the first author I'd read that admitted her flaws in great detail, and this inspired me. She revealed in one book that she was tired of people writing to her expecting something.

So I wrote to her and sent a small drawing of her garden from a photograph I'd seen. I included a card describing how she had inspired me already with her books, and I expected nothing in return.

Some months later I received an inspiring letter from May Sarton, thanking me for being so inspiring to her.

Do you inspire yourself?

Would you describe yourself as inspiring? Why/Why not?

The fact is, we are all capable of being inspired and inspiring. It is only our belief systems that stop us from being seen as inspiring. We believe we aren't inspiring! We are quick to point to others for that. We admire or idealize or want to emulate people we consider inspiring, yet to bestow that description on ourselves would be TOO BOLD somehow.

It's almost as if someone needs to describe us this way before we can be inspiring.

Begin now to ask friends if they find you inspiring. If they do, ask them "in which ways specifically?"

Make a list: Turn it into a poster for your wall. Add to it. Continue growing as an inspiring person.

If your friends don't find you inspiring, consider finding new friends

Ask yourself if YOU find YOU inspiring, and in what ways specifically. Make a list. Turn it into a poster.

I find myself inspiring in the following ways:

my quirky habits

my moving according to energy and flow

my dreams

my adventures

my miracle walks

my inventions

my literature

my ordinarily unusual friendships

my lifestyle

Magnify your experiences of inspiring people and things. Use the results to feed your creative dreams.

I am often inspired by the people who post on my "Marvelous Message Board" on my websight. Here is a message that inspired me while I was writing this book:

TOPIC: I went out with a Bosnian prince and a jewel smuggler

Since I have moved here, to the mountains that are so eerily beautiful and vague at the same time, I have been a relative recluse . . . ((healing))

But recently I have been meeting the most eclectic group of people.

I have met a pilot, a professor, a prince, a jewel smuggler, a poet, a professional photographer. I have met a 78-year-old potter, a writer.

!

I have seen and felt the land like I have at no other time.

I went to an Indian reservation, to one of the biggest lakes in the desert in the world (if you can imagine that). I took black-and-white photographs of a poet who was drinking red wine. The water was so soft and alkaline it felt like silk. We watched the thunderheads roll in, and it was an electric lightning show for hours. Then it was on to the shooting stars, too many to possibly count.

I have met people here in the Marvelous Message Board too. I have some new friends from all over the world. Letters are coming.

I am writing profusely—granted, it might be in the middle of the night, but at least it's coming out. I can say my insomnia is creating something!

Mars is the closest it has been to earth in 70,000 years.

There is so much creativity and movement in my life right now, so much growth and energy, I had to share.

I drank Turkish coffee last night in miniature porcelain cups with gold—while a man who speaks 10 languages fluently (including Latin) gazed upon my toe rings.

It is nice to feel another's watchful eye, when they are being gentle and respectful.

I have not had physical contact with any of the intriguing men I have been meeting, and that, my friends, is the most empowering feeling.

Blessings to you all—

I am going to go out on the playa this weekend (black rock desert) and pretend to be a desert princess who has to find her way home. I am going to wear a veil, and dance naked in the swelter of the sun. I am going to paint my body with dust and I am going to find the shade of a sagebrush to lay my body under, and I will whisper into the night of the secrets of the universe I have yet to comprehend.

Truly, this is a magical time.

Last night I held a small chunk of almost pure carbon from a meteorite that is 4 billion years old.

SHAKTIGIRL

Fabulous Fifth Month

Creative Dream Support Systems

week one

A Game or Something to Try

Ask a Friend for Support in a New Way

THINK OF SOMETHING that would benefit you or your creative dream. Maybe it's a neck massage, homemade soup, or going to a museum. Describe exactly what feels supportive to you, and be detailed and meticulous in this description. Ask your friend to fulfill your request and practice receiving it. We can all learn to expand our capabilities as receivers of support.

Offer a Friend Support in a New Way

THINK OF SOMETHING that could benefit your friend or their creative dream. Maybe it's a collage-making date, an adventure walk, or a foot massage. Contact your friend in an unusual way to extend this offer, perhaps by chalk on her sidewalk or serenading outside her window.

A G I F T for You

week two

I SEND YOU . . .

A sturdy platform of support. This platform is wide and strong and well made. It appears whenever you need it.

You climb easily onto the platform and realize that you are completely supported from every direction, and in every way. While on this platform, you also experience a deep sense of your own support for yourself.

This feeling of self-support increases whenever you think of your sturdy platform, and it is undiminished by fear, doubt, or loneliness.

You are also able to offer this sturdy platform of support to others who may need it. You realize that there is an infinite supply of support, and you experience it consistently.

"Give me a place to stand and I will move the earth" Archimedes

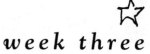

week three

A Positive Challenge (I Dare You)

Create a support section in your creative dream guidebook or a notebook.

> Make a list of who has been, or might be, supportive in your life. List ways to contact them.
>
> Write a description of what support means to you.
>
> Describe something or someone that feels supportive to you.
>
> What improvements might be needed in your support system?
>
> What kinds of support are you willing to provide to others?
>
> What kinds of support does your creative dream need?

You can turn to this section when you want to increase your feelings of support, or feel unsupported (by others or yourself).

Continue adding to this section as you and your dreams grow and develop.

week four

RADIANT Resources

You Can Heal Your Life
Louise Hay

Creating Money
Sanaya Roman and Duane Packer

Mozart Effect: Tapping the Power of Music to Heal the Body, Strengthen the Mind, and Unlock the Creative Spirit
Don Campbell

The Magic Cottage Address Book
SARK

Spilling Open: The Art of Becoming Yourself
Sabrina Ward Harrison

Harold and the Purple Crayon
Crockett Johnson

This Time I Dance: Trusting the Journey of Creating the Work You Love
Tama J. Kieves

Women of Spirit: Stories of Courage from the Women Who Lived Them
Katherine Martin

www.jengray.com
www.thework.org
www.writers.com
www.coping.org

CHAPTER SIX.

Sublime
Sixth Month

Committing to Your Dream and Keeping It Moving

The purpose of this chapter is to strengthen your commitment to your creative dream and find out more about time and what keeps dreams moving.

Have You Made a Commitment to Your Creative Dreams?

A COMMITMENT IS A PLEDGE OR PROMISE and is in effect even if we don't want it to be.

Creative dreams are messy and tangled and require focus and commitment to make them real.

Having the creative dream is very important. **Making it real is a choice** and involves commitment.

Commitment is what shelters and nourishes our dreams when we are crabbily avoiding, or once again procrastinating, or hiding from beginning because of our perfectionism.

YOU CAN CHOOSE to commit to a particular creative dream and change that dream as you explore and discover the nature of it.

Your original commitment is the basis for strength. If you commit to fulfilling your creative dreams, you can return to that commitment over and over again for energy and enthusiasm when your choices lead you into traps, challenges, or dead ends.

Creative dreams change all the time. We fulfill them, outgrow them, or simply lose interest.

Our commitment to having creative dreams can be made stronger by:

REASSESSING: How, or are, your creative dreams serving you? What do you or your creative dreams need at this time?

RECOMMITTING: Examine and explore your commitment. Has it shifted or changed? Do you need a new type or level of commitment?

Another way to recommit is to ask for others to become involved in your creative dream. You can do this by working with a team or a group, or by sending out an announcement

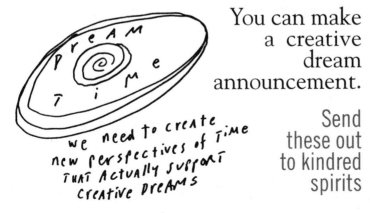

DreAM TiMe

we need to create new perspectives of Time ThAT ActuAlly support CreAtive DreAMs

You can make a creative dream announcement.

Send these out to kindred spirits

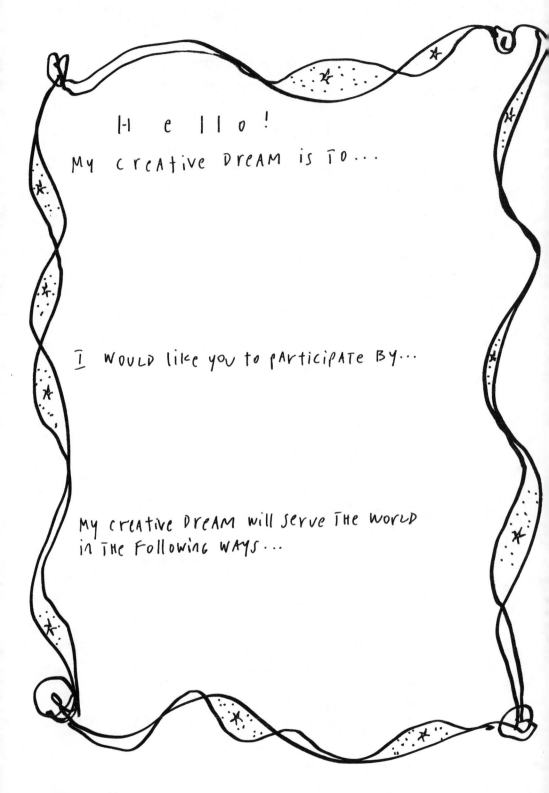

H e llo!

MY cREAtive DREAM is To...

I WOULD like you to pARticipAte By...

MY cREAtive DREAM will serve The World
in The Following WAYs...

Time and Creative Dreams

ONE OF THE BIGGEST CHALLENGES to commitment and to **keeping dreams moving is time.**

MOST OF US DO NOT HAVE UNLIMITED TIME for our creative dreams. Life is full of appointments, food preparation, missed buses, and interrupted sleep. Our work claims much of our time—family and friends claim the rest. It's only natural that we put our creative dreams aside "until there's more time."

So how can we keep our commitment to our creative dreams when "there's no time?"

We can change our perspective of time and realize that it's flexible and elastic.

When we are really busy, it appears that time is limited and inflexible. We say, "Well, there's only so many hours in the day."

We continue "proving" that time is "not on our side" by saying things like:

"There's a lot more I'd do with my creative dreams if I had more time."

We become overwhelmed by choosing too many activities and trying to wedge them into our lives.

I propose choosing a new attitude about time as it relates to your creative dreams.

We think we don't have time for our creative dreams because we continuously think that we must make large efforts.

The idea of these large efforts keep us from doing anything at all. Our commitment is strengthened in the moments, not in the hours.

Keeping Dreams Moving

The fact is:

Creative dreams will multiply with very small amounts of effort applied over time.

It is our creative dream idea that must be protected and kept fresh.

How do we do this?

Stop

Telling ourselves that time is:

Limited
Short
Scarce

Start

A program of micromovements to keep our creative dreams moving.

Keep

Your creative dreams active and visible by speaking about them or writing about them.

Develop

Your creative dream community by asking others to share their creative dreams and sharing yours.

Create

A visual map or plan of one of your creative dreams. Add micromovements that you think of.

But what if you feel too busy to do any of these things?

Most of us are.

Realize that you are
Not the only one

IT IS EASY TO IDEALIZE OTHERS and imagine them zipping along with their creative dreams and ideas. The truth is, most of us are not zipping along.

Most of us are muddling along, forgetting to return library books and searching for the cleanest socks to wear.

It is not so much about doing micromovements as it is thinking about doing them. If you bring your awareness to a new area, it will have an effect.

Anything new that you think about or do, is movement.

That movement can be incredibly tiny and incremental, and it will have an effect on our creative dreams.

I frequently forget all of this and become convinced of time scarcity and the failure of my ability to create movement. I have creative dreams that lie flat and forgotten. I hear myself say how overwhelmed I am and that it seems that "There just isn't enough time."

When this happens, it is time for new movement of some kind.

WHILE WRITING THIS BOOK, I began the rewrites and felt very overwhelmed and pressured by the amount of work that there was to do.

I also developed allergies in both eyes, a mysterious tooth pain, and was worried about my 80-year-old-mother's health. On this particular day, I just sat there surrounded by piles of things to do and all of my concerns, feeling helpless. I also began questioning my original commitment and wondered if I would be able to do all the work.

I decided that doing the laundry might help, and stomped across the street with 5 loads. When I got there, I noticed that I hadn't brought enough quarters and sighed with frustration. For some reason at that moment, I looked up.

There at the top of the wall near the ceiling, balanced on a pipe, was a stuffed blue dinosaur.

I just gasped with delight. It seemed to me that within that split second of seeing that blue dinosaur that all things were possible. I knew that someone had climbed up there and placed this stuffed animal, and that also thrilled me. I saw my neighbor Jimmie, and beckoned him inside to see the blue dinosaur. I told him about my bad mood and feeling

THe BIue DinoSAur

overwhelmed and pressured, and we shared experiences of coping with loss and change, and of the basic utterly helpless feelings that sometimes envelop us.

I came back later to get my clothes out of the washing machines, and saw with amazement a potted flowering plant on top of each washing machine. Jimmie had put these flowers there as gifts for me. Later, I came back to get my clothes out of the dryers and met the gentleman who cleans and maintains the machines. He exclaimed about the flowers and I asked him about the blue dinosaur. He said,

"I put it up there in case it could cheer someone up."

I explained how much it had cheered me, and how it had led to the flowers and a deep conversation. I then handed him one of the flowering plants. "Here, this one's for you."

He had tears in his eyes and said, "I've never had a plant before. How do you take care of it?"

We talked about not overwatering, and he walked off with his little red flower in a pot.

I went back to my writing filled with fresh commitment and new ideas. I decided that further movement was needed, and took everything out of my writing room. I stacked books, swept, vacuumed, moved furniture, and burned fresh sage. When I was finished, the room felt transformed. There were new plants, candles, and pieces of art from other rooms, and I just stood smiling, ready to create.

LARGE ATTITUDE CHANGES CAN HAPPEN in very small amounts of time. We continually forget this. I'm here to re-mind us.

I think that we are repeatedly tested and challenged with our commitments, to give us a chance to recommit, over and over again.

Creative dream making involves movement

Try this:

Write project ideas on index cards

Throw the index cards into the air

Pick the first one you see to work with

We can make our creative dreams visible by our movements Often, making is made of simple things:

organizing   moving   shuffling

rearranging   taking out

opening   putting away

EVERY TIME I WRITE A BOOK, I am reminded of how much of it involves moving papers around. Stacking, placing, paper-clipping, arranging, rearranging.

I make it real by making it move

When I can make it move, I can see my original commitment in action.

Movement assists every creative dream in becoming real.

Remember: the gift of inertia is the absence of movement.

When we physically move, it changes patterns of energy and shifts the way our brain works.

You can also do a lot with the visualization of movement if you're physically not able to move.

We can use all of our senses to activate our creative dreams and create movement. We can:

sing

clap

stretch

BOUNCE

skip

You can let these movements lead you into creative dream-making activity:

Sing before studying

Clap before playing music

Stretch before painting

Bounce before writing

Skip before sculpting

MY PRAYER FOR THIS BOOK is that it gives strength and shelter to people and their creative dreams.

It is bold to live and speak about creative dreams, and it **involves daring.** Many of us fall into silence and passivity and use time as the reason, but how are we actually using our time?

I invite you to live your creative dreams and make them real for others to share.

The world endows you with this power and awakens you to your purpose. We are all really much more than we think, our actions can be splendidly imperfect, and we can avoid our creative dreams and still have an effect. Movements are more important than results in the case of dreams.

A Review

IN ORDER TO EXPLORE your commitment and to keep your creative dreams moving, let's review what we've discussed and your experiences so far.

Refer back to each section or just answer from memory

(If you're reading straight through, you can come back to this later.)

Finding and Naming Your Dream(s)
CHAPTER ONE

Page 24

Did you choose or name your dream?

What is it?

If you're not sure, can you make one up?

The Land of No

CHAPTER TWO

Page 42

How much time do you spend in the Land of No?

Did you learn anything new by reading or thinking about this land?

If so, what?

Have you tried any of the suggestions?

If not, what would you try first if you did try?

The World of Yes

CHAPTER THREE

Page 67

Who are your allies, teachers, or mentors?

How much or often do you experience self-acceptance?

How much time do you spend in the World of Yes?

Have you tried any of the suggestions?

If so, which one or ones?

Making Creative Dreams Real with MicroMOVEments

CHAPTER FOUR

Page 88

Have you chosen one or more? Why or why not?

What is your micromovement about this?

What do you like or dislike about micromovements?

Creative Dream Support Systems

CHAPTER FIVE

Page 105

How much support do you feel with regard to your creative dreams?

Have you had any experiences of increased support? If so, what were they?

Can you describe your support systems right now?

Be aware that you might be the type of person who doesn't review in this way. As a result, you might not have done any of the suggestions in this book. This is perfectly okay and doesn't mean you are not growing, learning, or changing.

Your style of movement may be different. Can you describe it?

New Perspectives and Possible Changes

NOW IT'S TIME for new perspectives and possible changes in how you're using this book. This is part of a strengthening your commitment or reassessing it.

Are you reading only?

How does this inspire and/or help you with your creative dreams?

Are you reading and doing activities and experiences?

How does this assist you with your creative dreams?

Are you a dabbler, picking it up when you need a burst of energy?

How does this assist you with your creative dreams?

Have you barely looked at it and wonder how it could possibly assist you?

How does this assist you with your creative dreams?

Do you feel like the only one who doesn't have time or energy to spend on their creative dreams?

How does this assist you with your creative dreams?

Exploring your way of learning and moving is a way of making your commitment stronger. Can you identify and describe your commitment to your creative dreams?

Books are like doorways or windows into other ways of being. This book is a friendly opening. It will patiently wait for your whole self to move, grow, and change.

I encourage you not to make progress until the time feels right. When the timing is right, things move differently. What was previously difficult becomes exceedingly easy. **There is no right way to use this book.** There is no timetable that is best. There are only the questions.

Are you living your creative dreams?
Why or why not?

Sublime Sixth Month

Committing to Your Dream and Keeping it Moving

week one

A Game or Something to Try

Field Trip for Your Creative Brain

GO TO THE BOOKSTORE, library, or museum for the sheer purpose of being inspired. Look at books or images you've never looked at before, at subjects that normally don't interest you. This literally changes your brain chemistry.

Find something brand-new, juicy, and unexpected.
Tell someone about what you discovered or write it down.

A G I F T for You

I SEND YOU . . .

A brand-new clock and calendar. Your new clock
is the clock of forgiveness. It doesn't KEEP time, but GIVES it
to you in the kindest measure. If you are feeling rushed or
pressured, time slows down. If you are late and don't wish to
be, time goes backward. (For skeptics, this clock secretly
changes so that the mind doesn't know it.)

Your new calendar is the calendar of abundance. There are
as many or few days as you wish, and the days are adjusted to
your mood and personality. This calendar fills up or empties,
based on what feels best to you.

You consult your forgiving clock and calendar of abundance
with great humor and delight.

You realize that time is entirely your perception, and there
is always enough.

You begin noticing more and more how everything is really
perfectly timed.

☆

week three

A Positive Challenge (I Dare You)

TELL YOUR CREATIVE DREAM to someone you don't know
well or know at all.

This could be anyone you meet in your daily life. Find a
way to bring it up and have a little discussion if possible.
Maybe you will find out about his or her creative dream!

'THE FUTURE BELONGS TO THOSE WHO BELIEVE IN THE BEAUTY OF THEIR DREAMS'
eleanor roosevelt

What do you say quickly about your creative dream? This will show you more about the core of your dream. It could also feel awkward or forced, or could feel too shy to do it at all. This is O.K., you can just try on another day.

Or,

Say your creative dream out loud on a walk, just to hear it in the air.

week four

RADIANT Resources

Walking in This World: The Practical Art of Creativity
Julia Cameron

*I Promise Myself: Making a Commitment to Yourself
and Your Dreams*
Patricia Lynn Reilly

The Call: Discovering Why You're Here
Oriah Mountain Dreamer

Play! Book and Journal: A Place to Dream While Awake
SARK

*The Lost Soul Companion: A Book of Comfort and Constructive
Advice for Struggling Artists, Black Sheep, Square Pegs,
and Other Free Spirits*
Susan M. Brackney

*Tracks: A Woman's Solo Trek Across 1,700 Miles
of Australian Outback*
Robyn Davidson

Forget Perfect: Finding Joy, Meaning, and Satisfaction in the Life You've Already Got and the You You Already Are
  Lisa Earle McLeod and Joann Swan Neely

The Essential Rumi
  Coleman Barks

www.exerciseplus.com
www.awakeningartistry.com
www.inspirationpeak.com
www.lostsoulcompanion.com
www.hedgebrook.org

CHAPTER SEVEN

Superb
Seventh Month

Inspiring Stories and Examples of Creative Dreams and Dreamers

The purpose of this chapter is to connect you with other people and their creative dream experiences. This gives you a virtual dream community to inspire your creative dreams.

My Creative Dreams and What I've Learned

BECAUSE I AM LIVING MY CREATIVE DREAM of being an artist and writer, people sometimes think that I have fulfilled all of my creative dreams. I have so many creative dreams! Here are some of the ones I've made real so far:

Living in Europe

Riding a bicycle 3,000 miles

Living on islands

Living in a "Magic Cottage"

Sharing my life with a cat

My Bike was named MAX

MY
House
of Dreams
HAS
Many levels and
lAYers

Creating a company

Mentoring people

Contributing money and services to others

Owning a home

Writing and publishing 12 books

Creating art

Writing two children's books

Working with a personal and business coach

Working with a psychotherapist

Becoming self-employed and working at home

Becoming an Irish citizen

Loving and being loved by close, intimate friends

Every one of these creative dreams shared the same obstacles:

Fear

Inner critics

Outer critics

Lack of money

Lack of experience
Perfectionism
Procrastination
Avoidance

The truth is, you just bring your obstacles along on your creative dream-making journey. Don't wait to solve them before making your creative dreams real. If you wait to solve them, you will wait a very long time, because new obstacles will always pop up and the old obstacles will change shape. I have entered all of my creative dreams in various states of disarray and dishevelment. This is good.

OBSTACLES LIKE TO HANG OUT IN TANGLES AND TRICK US INTO NOT SEEING THE SURPRISES

THESE STATES ARE A KIND OF TEST. How much do you believe in your creative dream or want it to become real? If you turn back because of fear, you will continually be turning back.

Turning back is not bad when it's a choice, but often turning back is a form of misguided self-protection.

If I turn back now, I won't have to _____ or _____.

Making your creative dreams real requires you to be involved, inspired, and forward-moving even when you feel none of these things. Especially when you feel blocked, lost, and crabby and like hiding most of all.

WE ALL DREAM of the perfect mentor, miraculous funding, an "angel" to come and help us, an award, a grant, a scholarship, a business loan. While some of these may come along to assist you, most likely you will be alone with your creative dreams, cobbling together makeshift plans.

YOU MIGHT CALL, write e-mail, ask, advertise, make lists, dream, plan, scheme, ask again, read, research, and study ways for your creative dreams to become real.

With regard to making my creative dreams real, I've been:

rejected	betrayed
ridiculed	guided
stagnant	immensely supported
misinformed	mentored
successfully unsuccessful	invested in
copied	assisted

Because I have published a book a year, I am described as prolific. I have barely begun to be prolific.

There is so much to dream!

I have experienced the following with regard to my dreams:

euphoria

fulfillment

frustration

betrayal

loss

satisfaction

ecstasy

JUST KEEP on experiencing

I have mismanaged my dreams, made naive mistakes, forgotten that I'm fallible and supremely flawed, and made poor choices and decisions about living my dreams.

I have fallen and bounced.

I have been flattened and crushed and encountered searing pain. I misjudged other people who were involved with my dreams. I misjudged myself about my dreams.

I quit over and over.

I began again.

All the while, I continued dreaming.

Someone called my inspiration line and asked,

"How did you find your dreams?
How did they look so beautiful?"

QUITTING
is
NOT DEFEAT

They didn't look beautiful at all once I began them.
From a distance, there was beauty. Close up, I saw all of
my ugly doubts and limitations.

I flailed.
I say to you all
Flail more!

It's in flailing that the dreams gain their beauty. When
we handle our dreams they can become "love-rubbed."
I invite you to make all the mistakes I made. I regret nothing.
Well, perhaps that I haven't lived even more of my dreams . . .
I intend for this book to support and nourish each one of my
dreams, and awaken me to even more dreaming.

May our creative dreams swirl around us all of
our days and nights. May we be like
naked stars with our
creative dreams.

Naked star:

A majority of its gaseous atmosphere stripped away, because of its encounters with other stars.

cute little naked star

Here are some of my currently active and inactive creative dreams:

Building and living in a treehouse

Going on a photographic safari in Africa

Adopting a child

Writing/creating a novel

Exhibiting my art

Living in Ireland

Creating a foundation for arts programs in the schools

Revisioning elder-care systems

Having my own radio show

Writing a screenplay

Living with and having a lover/partner

Being at peace with my body

You can be certain that I will be flailing, experimenting, succeeding, and avoiding all of these dreams.

I'D LIKE TO INTRODUCE you to a group of people who answered my creative dream questions. I chose to interview friends for this particular book, so it is not a random sampling of people but an idiosyncratic combination of dear souls, all with valuable thoughts to share about creative dreams. I chose friends with particular kinds of work and dreams in order to provide as many different perspectives as possible.

REMEMBER AS YOU "MEET" these creative dreamers within these pages that you might find yourself comparing or even feeling left out. This is splendidly human and very understandable.

Please know that if you answered my creative dream questionnaire, and I put you into this book, that others would find you equally inspiring.

In fact, I am requesting that you consider answering my questions on page 163 and put yourself into this book. If it's a library book, please make your own page separately.

If you're uncomfortable answering questions by yourself, ask a friend to send them to you. Include a photograph and include yourself. If we meet, I'd like to see "your" page.

I am reminded that each of our dreams touches another's dreams. We don't all need to travel or write books or have babies in order to touch these experiences.

Clark, ARTIST

www.clarktate.com

Do you have a creative dream or dreams?

I want to be successful at creating cartoon furniture, character sculptures, children's books, and animated shows.

Does anything stop or scare you with regard to your creative dreams?

I am often scared by the forward motion of a possible dream, when it begins to come to life. Maybe that's my fear of pending failure . . . or even fear of what success might mean. Either way, it's scary.

What inspires or excites you about creative dreams?

Sometimes there's what I call "energized bliss." I'm excited when I'm pulled into the flow of something bigger than myself. It's this energy that surrounds the piece of work. I have to let go of control and yet stay a part of it in a conscious way.

Would you describe yourself as living your creative dream or dreams?

I'd describe myself as wrestling with my creative dream . . . and in some worlds, wrestling IS living. What I personally tend to do is feel constantly on the brink of making something happen. And then I am absolutely disappointed in myself if it doesn't get done. Like being aware of that "window of time" after it's closed. Don't get me wrong, I believe I live a creative life. Just not exactly the dream part.

What might help you to live more of your creative dreams?

My mother recently said to me, "Don't just think. Do." I keep this in front of my drawing board and see it every day . . . and try my best to understand this foreign language. Another possibility is to find the bliss and then see how that creates the dream. I just thought of this . . . so I have no idea if it works.

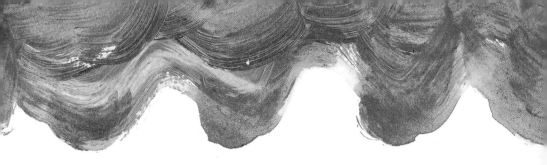

Describe in detail one of your creative dreams.

I'm in the midst of writing a children's book. I'm polishing a final draft. I've completed two paintings representing style, and completed sketches for the rest. I'm nearly ready to send it to an agent or a publisher . . . and I'm STALLED there. Stuck. Like I'm some leaf caught in the swirling eddy of a stream. I think I've just described my reality part of the dream.

What have you done to live your creative dreams?

Sidestepped a former career and walked away from a stable paycheck. I closed my eyes and hoped everything would work out. I was a creative director at an ad agency, and am now a freelance illustrator. This was my way of stretching closer to my dream so the crossover was within my reach. I'm reminded of the man who said, "You can't buy happiness . . . but you can buy a big boat that can sail right up next to it."

What are you willing to do?

Work long hours. Listen to good advice. Stretch my shy, resistant, self-selling side. And try to never give up.

Can you imagine your creative dream helping the world? If so, how?

It would be great if children created a stronger self-image from something I had done, written, or drawn. Found some message that helped them through a difficult time. That would be really fulfilling.

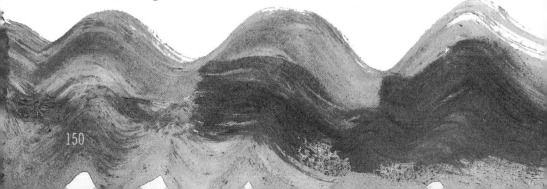

Elissa, COPY EDITOR

www.artandletters.com

Do you have a creative dream?

Develop my photography practice and bring my photographs into the world.

Does anything scare or stop you?

The difficulty of finding time to work on it, and giving it a lower priority than my obligations (work, etc.). Also, sometimes I give my work less value because I'm not the very best photographer in the world, so what's the point? (This happens when I listen to my inner critics.)

What inspires or excites you about your creative dream?

My photographs are an expression of who I am as a unique individual, and they give the opportunity to express my gifts. They bring pleasure to people and can even bring solace. And they're fun to carry out.

Would you describe yourself as living your creative dreams?

I've taken a few baby steps toward it, but again, there never seems to be time.

What would help you in living more of your creative dream?

Not having to work for a living! But probably more important, being less self-critical and trusting that my creative work is of value and deserving of my time and effort.

What have you done to live your creative dreams?

Taken lots of pictures. Given photographs to friends. Donated photographs to charity benefits. Done some investigation of cafés that show photographs. Found a local camera club. Found a good framer. Started taking more photographs. Started bringing my camera with me when I go out. Taken steps to set up a websight.

What advice would you give?

First, don't give up! If you don't have a lot of time, at least do a little bit as often as possible. Confide your dreams to supportive friends. Find creative buddies with whom you can work on your dreams together. Start giving away your creative work as soon as possible—as gifts, donations, and so on. The good response you get will build your confidence and your energy to do more. And the happiness your work brings people will make you feel wonderful. Also, develop solid counterarguments to your inner critics' misguided attempts to shield you from failure. (Here's an example: **Inner critic:** You're not the best_____ in the world, so you might as well not bother. **Me:** It's not a competition—my contribution is unique because it's coming from me, and I'm a unique individual. We all have a unique contribution to make.)

How or why are creative dreams important to you?

Because when I'm being creative, I feel like I'm expressing my true self.

John, TEACHER

What stops you from living your creative dream?

I think the main hindrance for me personally in making creative dreams real is a fear of making real choices. I've always believed, probably arrogantly and unrightly, that I could do anything I wanted. The problem is radical adherence to a choice: is my dream to be a highbrow writer or a vagabond traveler? One day it's one thing and the next it's another.

In not choosing, there is a kind of freedom that choosing precludes. This is obviously destructive and immature. I'm working on it.

There is also a mentality I was raised with that emphasizes stability in regard to job and income. I'm by no means blaming the upbringing, it's just difficult to change one's way of thinking. Being in a relationship with someone who has realized her creative dreams and grew up in an environment that encouraged them is both inspiring and intimidating. The story of my partner's dad, who went through years of poverty and uncertainty, but never wavered from his dream, is also inspiring and intimidating. I have a history of giving up on things, so it's challenging to try to emulate someone who didn't.

Another obstacle (assuming that we can follow the logic of the world of created obstacles) that I personally feel is a lack of calling. I've always envied people who knew there was one thing they were put on this world to do. At times, I've had dreams ranging from rock star to geologist, teacher to fireman. And those notions were all in my adult life! Recently!

Has your creative dream changed with time?

> As I get older, my dream gets smaller: a job with some element of creative/intellectual dynamism, something meaningful, as in contributing to the betterment of a community (as a younger person I would have said "society," but that seems too ambitious now), and an income decent enough that I could take my girl on a swingin' date every so often.

> A small dream, to be built on quite probably if and when it occurs.

NOTE: *As I completed this book, John fulfilled a creative dream and took a job teaching in China for a year.*

Jason Purcell,

ARTIST

Do you have a creative dream?

> I have devoted my thoughts and actions to manifesting a life as an artist specifically working in abstract mixed media painting, as well as a Souful speaker on many forms of creative manifestation and peak performance. Through persistence and passion (and a lot of teaching and speaking on what I needed to learn), I have exhibited my work in New York, Japan, and across the United States, fulfilling many of the dreams and visions I first felt compelled to pursue in 1990.

Does anything stop or scare you?

It is my experience that "we are the questions we ASK!" I am constantly examining the questions I ask myself. . . . Do the questions empower/inspire me to trust in myself fully, or are they simply another form of scarcity thinking which ab-SOUL-utely serves no purpose at this time in my life. Also, sometimes when we LEAP, the net doesn't appear!!! Sometimes we are supposed to celebrate the freefall, hit the ground hard, and get back up. Ultimately, the net will be the foundation of consciousness that supports our Creative Leaps. First, celebrate and never lose the constant courage to Leap. Second, build yourself the best damn net/rope/bungee cord you can that allows you to constantly jump similing into the unknown territory.

What inspires or excites you about your creative dream?

The powerful magic of any creative or spiritual practice is in the doing, the surrender of ego and the willingness to be led by your highest vision without the burden ofjudgment. The artist's job is to create . . . passionately! Saying "yes" over and over! I am excited about being fully alive and engaged with my Creative Dreams. I see the results of a commitment to speaking the truth in all facets of my life and a cultivation of a knowing born from asking the powrful question "How may I Serve?" At some point during the day I ask this question . . . paying attention to the answer. In doing so, a fantastic epiphany of trust resonates in my life which has allowed me (most days) to stop grasping and start listening deeply to my spirit's desires and fascinations. Moreover, I have learned to focus on excellence in my craft while letting go of the results, creating with a great humility and love for the process.

Would you describe yourself as living your creative dream?

YES!!!

Do you think that living one dream stops you or slows you down from living others?

Good question. First, let's establish the Big Dream and make sure our "Creative Belief Detector System" is ON. Ultimately, how we live our life is the highest art form and the message we embody to our family, friends, and the World in which we Live. Second, knowing this and the qualities of experience we seek to create allows for a more intuitive body-centered approach to living our creative dreams. Each dream we have is at a different stage of development and has different needs. Ask yourself this question: "How may I serve this dream now?" This simple question will cultivate a deeper trust in your path and limit the amount of excuses you try to sell yourself. Our dreams are born, walk, and finally run off into the world with the strength and quality of the attention we infuse in them. Knowing this we are better prepared to understand the stage of development and level of attention and commitment each soulful desire calls for.

What advice would you give?

I have always like the phrase "if you want more joy in your life, tell the truth quicker." The truth is always the starting point, and when we cultivate that knowing, our lives and actions become a great gift to the world. Dare to Shine!

Val, EXPRESSIVE ARTS THERAPIST

www.valtate.com

Do you have a creative dream?

As an expressive arts therapist utilizing various art modalities, I want to help adults remember how to play, rediscover their innate artistic nature, recognize their truths, and trust in their own creative path of life. At some point, I also imagine working in an integrative health center as part of a healing arts team.

What inspires or excites you with regard to creative dreams?

To me, creative dreams in waking life are like lucid dreams in sleep. If we become conscious of our actions and intentions, the possibilities for manifestation are endless. Once I realized that societal expectations are simply one construct about how to live, I felt compelled to take over my own life. Creative dreams for me are about how I choose to live, rather than achieving a special goal.

What have you done to live your creative dreams?

I radically changed my career path. To do this, I had to admit to myself that my work in advertising was not satisfying my creative dream. Then I had to take a leap of faith that something else would. What I did to live my creative dream was to have faith, trust in myself, let go of my pride and attachment to being "accomplished," and accept that my life is a creative process.

What advice would you give to anyone about waiting to live his or her creative dreams?

Always remember that your life mission and path is uniquely your own. Learn to be your own mirror for what feels right and true. Listen to your intuition. You are the only one who knows your answers. Choose to surround yourself with people who support your creative dreams. Don't discount the road you have already traveled on. Each step brought you to right now.

What other creative dreams can you imagine doing or living?

I want to travel the world, do mission work, live in an artistic community, and breed dogs. Also, I want to take more painting, cooking, and drumming classes, learn to play the violin, adopt a puppy, run support groups for pregnant women and mothers, and be a conscious and loving mother myself.

Sabrina, ARTIST AND AUTHOR

www.sabrinawardharrison.com

Do you have a creative dream?

My first thought is, "No, I don't. I wish I did." I feel like I have a new one every day. A studio/stable, horses and art, in the country, then a flashy, sexy New York City life, then cozy family home with pink jasmine, the Italian wine seaside soaking life . . .

It goes on and on. I have come to realize more than anything, I want a soft, peaceful heart.

Does anything stop or scare you with regard to your creative dreams?

Thinking I'll commit to something I shouldn't. Regretting a decision I've made, for personal or financial reasons.

What inspires or excites you about creative dreams?

A full life. I am really quite dramatic; I like fullness. I like to feel life happening. I fear numbness and boredom. Sometimes, normal life really depresses me and scares me, yet, I crave "normal" so much.

Would you describe yourself as living your creative dream or dreams?

From many people's eyes, my life seems like one big creative dream. Not so much to me. I focus too much on the keeping it going, keeping up the pace, pressure on myself, to do more, check one more thing off a long to-do list. "Just get some health and car insurance . . . just get . . ."

What would help you to live more of your creative dreams?

A brilliant assistant/business manager. (I judge this answer. It doesn't sound too succulent, but if I have this, I can go draw in India.)

Can you imagine your creative dreams helping the world?

I could travel farther into the world, teach, paint, write, hear more stories of us human beings trying to figure this life out.

What advice would you give to anyone wanting to live his or her creative dreams?

Risk.
Leap.
Speak up.

Vanessa, STUDENT

OOOOOH—HOW EXCITING! More good SARK help for procrastinators like me! I'll answer your questions right away. In an effort to procrastinate other work.

Do you have creative dream or dreams?

Absolutely. Write great books (fiction and nonfiction) about travel, sex, discovery, adventure. Make ten three-inch-square canvasses that stay on the wall of a coffee house. Design my own home and creative work space. Dance with a traveling company.

Does anything stop or scare you with regard to your creative dreams?

I'm certain they're way too ambitious. I get lazy about the first steps—don't make the phone calls, don't turn the computer on, don't make time to paint. I worry that I'm going to try to do too much and therefore end up doing nothing, but I also don't want to only focus on one thing because I worry I'll get bored.

What inspires or excites you with regard to creative dreams?

I do have some glimmer of hope that I'll be able to make a few of them work. I look at journals from five, ten years ago and see that I've already accomplished some of my dreams—who's to say I won't accomplish more? When I was eleven, I wrote a list of things I wanted to do with my life. One of them was write—and I am. Slowly. I also get excited in those rare, beautiful moments when I actually do feel that I am creating something. I cling to those moments when the world feels tired and the future seems bleak.

Describe in detail one of your creative dreams (one you're currently engaged in or not yet engaged in).

I have been working on a small book for about a year. It is called *Fumblings and Adventure Stories*. It is gaining shape, but is still an infant, and I am tender about it. It is a sort of an interactive memoir, with stories from my life and questions/activities for readers. It will have a few black-and-white sketches, and hopefully will be published before I go to graduate school. The publishing part feels completely unreal, but I say it so that I'm accountable.

Would you describe yourself as living your creative dream or dreams?

Yes and no. I am working very hard toward arranging my life so that I can live my creative dreams and also eat every day. I spent a lot of time working at jobs that are not so creative to pay the bills, but I'm also changing that situation and taking off to Thailand, where I will stew in tropical awe until I've been inspired to be the artist that I wish I was now. I ache for more successes, more completion, and more sense of progress.

What are you willing to do for your dreams?

Quit my job, live more cheaply, dedicate most of my time, read a lot of books, go back to school, receive guidance/editing suggestions, disappoint those who have different expectations.

Kindred Spirits for Creative Dreams

WHEN WE READ ABOUT PEOPLE IN A BOOK, it's tempting to think, "But that's not me, and it's easier for them." It's also tempting to compare ourselves with other people. Don't do it! It's simply not true that you're less than anybody.

One of the reasons I am writing this book is to welcome you into a huge community of kindred spirits. Here are just 2 of the many responses I received when I asked people to post their creative dreams on my websight.

> *My creative dream is to celebrate who I am. I want to be able to feel comfortable in my own skin. I want to open my ears and my heart to everyone and close my mouth more. I want to perfect the art of "nodding," the technique of letting people know you're listening without saying a word. I want to be able to accept my downfalls, wrap my arms around them to remind myself that they are not so big. I want to be able to sit and be quiet, so that I may listen to what my inner voice is telling me. I want to paint freely and without reservation or fear of rejection. I want to be able to feed the dreams of others without doubt or hesitation. I want to be free of old shadows by learning to forgive. I want to learn to look strangers in the eyes and not fear the unknown. I want to learn to live every day and not let grand opportunities pass me by because of fear. I want to love myself and that is my creative dream.*
>
> FROM: JINNY

> *Creative dream*
> *My creative dream is to live every moment as a prayer.*
> FROM: BINDY JR.

Creative Dream Questions

I would like to know YOUR answers to the following questions:

Do you have a creative dream or dreams?

What is it/are they?

Does anything stop or scare you with regard to your creative dreams? If so, what?

What inspires or excites you with regard to creative dreams?

Would you describe yourself as living your creative dream or dreams? Why or why not?

If not, what do you think would help you live more of your creative dreams?

Do you think that the living of one dream stops you or slows you down from living others? If so, please explain.

Describe in detail one of your creative dreams (one you're currently engaged in or not yet engaged in).

What have you done to live your creative dreams?

What are you willing to do?

What advice would you give to anyone wanting to live his or her creative dreams?

Can you imagine your creative dream helping the world? If so, how?

What other creative dreams can you imagine doing or living?

How or why are your creative dreams important to you?

Describe yourself ultimately living one or more of your creative dreams.

Use this page to put in your answers and a photograph of yourself.

USe THiS PAGe To
tell Me your CreAtive DreAM Story

PHoto or DrAWiNG
of YoU

Superb Seventh Month

Inspiring Stories and Examples of Creative Dreams and Dreamers

A Game or Something to Try

HAVE A CREATIVE DREAM TEA PARTY OR GATHERING with friends (works best with 3 or more).

The purpose of this tea or gathering is to honor creative dreams and inspire the dreamers.

Ask each friend to make 6 cards. On the cards, list:

Their creative dream	An inspiring story
A fear or block about it	An offer of support
A support request	A success with their creative dream

Mix up the cards and have each person choose 6. Have each person read one card and respond. Eat and drink delicious things while discussing creative dreams.

A G I F T for You

I SEND YOU . . .
An Invitation to My House

Please consider virtually or telepathically attending my Creative Dream Tea Party. Please feel free to wear pajamas.

Come over just before the sun sets, and we'll watch the glow over the Golden Gate Bridge.

I'll use my cheerfully mismatched tea set and serve 2 kinds of tea: rooibos or honeybush for caffeine free, and double Earl Grey for caffeine. There will be soy milk and half-and-half. We'll use stevia for sweetener.

We'll snack on blackberries, dark chocolate, and shortbread cookies from Scotland.

We'll eagerly share creative dream stories and things we don't understand. Laughter will escort us into the evening time, and all the candles will be lit. We'll talk about everything and nothing, and lie around on couches and pillows, admiring the night sky. My cat, Jupiter, will bring news from the garden downstairs, and the scent of night-blooming jasmine.

Stories will tumble over each other and we'll be inspired long after our creative tea party ends.

week three

A Positive Challenge (I Dare You)

Make a list of creative dream-livers you admire.

Who are they?

What are their creative dreams?

What do you admire about them?

In what ways have you or the world benefited from their creative dreams made real?

Keep adding to this list. See if you'd like to "adopt" any as your allies for your creative dreams.

week four

RADIANT Resources

Be Here Now
Ram Dass

The Art of Possibility: Transforming Personal and Professional Life
Rosamund Stone Zander and Benjamin Zander

Inspiration Sandwich: Stories to Inspire Our Creative Freedom
SARK

Discover Your Genius: How to Think Like History's Ten Most Revolutionary Minds
Michael J. Gelb

Deep Play
  Diane Ackerman

The Art of Looking Sideways
  Alan Fletcher

How You Do Anything Is How You Do Everything
  Cheri Huber

The Creative Habit
  Twyla Tharp

Everyday Matters
  Danny Gregory

What Do We Know: Poems and Prose Poems
  Mary Oliver

*Book Lust: Recommended Reading for
Every Mood, Moment, and Reason*
  Nancy Pearl

www.thisamericanlife.com
www.superherodesigns.com
www.word-wrangler.com
www.herondance.org
www.dannygregory.com
www.swirlygirl.com

CHAPTER EIGHT

Ecstatic Eighth Month

Living Your Creative Dreams

The purpose of this chapter is to deal with the difficult parts of actually living your creative dreams.

Fear and Loss

HAVING AND LIVING your creative dreams will **awaken** and **activate** fears. This is to be expected and planned for. In order to deal with fear, you need to be able to:

Recognize and identify it.

Speak of it, write it down.

Establish the nature of it.

Ask is it rational, irrational, or a mixture.

Address the fears in some way.

Find solutions, ask for help or support.

Redirect the fears.

Figure out where fears can live, so you can continue moving in the direction you choose.

HOLD FAST TO DREAMS
For if DREAMS DIE
Life is A Broken-winGed Bird
THAT Cannot Fly.

Langston Hughes

When we recognize or identify a fear, it loses some of its power. I think that fears expand in isolation, that recognition and identification make them visible so that you can share fears with your community and receive support.

Establishing the nature of the fear dismantles it.

Is your fear:

ANTICIPATORY
What might, or could happen, "what if"
This includes trying to predict the future, or "futurizing"

IRRATIONAL
Wild imaginings, no basis in fact, "off the wall"

CATASTROPHIZING
The worst, most awful things you can imagine

RATIONAL
Factual, actual, something that is real

Addressing the fear is a powerful way to work with it
and lessen its impact. When we can share a fear in some way, it doesn't weigh as much or press so heavily. Asking for support with a fear that means we are no longer alone with our

experience. This is also a good way to find out that we are not the only ones who have this particular fear.

Redirecting fears means moving them around so they are not blocking or impeding your progress.

You might:

Create a holding place for fears in the form of a box or an envelope. Put your fears on paper and put them here. You can think differently about a fear when it is not just inside your head.

Set your fears on fire. Write them down and burn them up. This is a process of liberating and separating you from your fears.

Ask a friend to hear your fears first without comment or solution. Then if you feel ready, ask for suggestions and feedback for one thing you could do to redirect your fear.

Another way to work with fear is to study your own fear patterns.

Are your fears:

TEMPORARY
Fleeting, brief

LONG-STANDING
Deep, predictable

UNPREDICTABLE
You don't know until you're experiencing it

Do you respond to fears by:

DENYING
"Oh there's nothing to be afraid of."

MINIMIZING

"Oh I'm a little scared, but it's not a big deal."

DWELLING

"I've always been afraid of this and let me explain why, and I'll never get over it."

OBSESSING

"But what about _____? I just keep thinking about _____."

MOVING THROUGH

"Yes, I'm scared and I'm doing it anyway."

GETTING STUCK

"It's too scary, I'm quitting."

ALONG WITH OUR FEARS, comes loss. As dreams are fulfilled or change shape, there are losses as well as successes.

There is certainly more attention paid to dream successes, yet the losses are part of what made those successes.

Erin speaks beautifully about loss:

> *In response to SARK's wanting to hear about what our "dreams" are, this is what I'd like to say:*
>
> *In my life now, before I begin to build new dreams, I wish fervently that I may be able to find a place within myself in which to honor the tremendous losses of my dreams today.*
>
> *I don't know that I'm personally equipped to a) face and b) accept the fact that many of the dreams I have spent building have now crumbled down around me.*
>
> *I'd like to see a place develop within myself in which I can honor the loss of those dreams—a dream cradle if you will—and then find another place within myself in which I can begin to build new dreams.*

I hope that as a society we can learn to find a place within ourselves and each other to honor the loss of old dreams and the birthing of new ones.

FROM: ERIN HURME

Doing More Things Badly

ONE OF THE MOST inhibiting factors for creative dream-living is how often we think we need to do something well or perfectly to begin it. Many of us procrastinators rehearse something new in our minds so often that we completely drain ourselves of energy to begin it at all. Many of us perfectionists don't try at all until it can be "done right."

One of my dreams is to feel at peace with my body. I've had a long history of struggle and conflict with my body (as many of us have) and this year I was determined start a new exercise program.

This sounds easy when you read about it or think about it, but it's quite a different matter when you actually have to do it.

None of my previous attempts with body changes had worked very well for very long, so I decided to try a different approach: I gave myself permission to do an exercise program badly.

When I hired a personal trainer, I explained that I didn't want to spend too much money or time on exercise, and that I did want to be inspired, encouraged, and delighted by the experience. She agreed to create a program with me and my moods in mind, and we started working together.

We invented games to play that used my muscles, but also made me laugh.

I then invented other ways to exercise by myself. I did:

Tai chi on the treadmill

Boxing while riding a bike

Bouncing on giant balls

Lifting weights while singing

At first I met with her once a week, but soon I felt inspired to come twice a week. If I had tried to start with 2 times a week, I know that I would have quit.

Someone called my **inspiration phone** line and told me about a book called *The Diet Cure*. That day I went shopping at the natural food store and a book fell off the shelf in front of my shopping cart. I picked up the book and saw the title, *The Diet Cure*. I took it home and quickly decided to begin the program described in the book. It's a 12-week program and I didn't have time to do all the things outlined, so I called for an appointment anyway and requested a different schedule, spread out over 6 months. After I explained what I needed, the people at the diet cure program supported my choice and worked with me at a slower pace.

If I waited until I "had time" to do this program it would have never happened. I want to give you **permission** and **encouragement** to **experiment with doing more things badly.**

What does your creative dream need and how might you do it badly just to begin?

You might:

Sign up for a class and only go once.

Join a team and then back out when or if it doesn't help you.

Start learning something and quit.

Perhaps you are wondering how these suggestions could possibly be helpful. Remember that **simply starting**

something new will lead you into experiences and places you haven't been before. These new experiences and places will cause new growth.

You can then use this new growth for your creative dream-living.

We can liberate ourselves to do more things badly, partially, or not at all. We can refuse to feel guilty about this too.

Rebelling and Nonconforming

ONE OF THE DIFFICULTIES with living your creative dreams is how society encourages and supports conforming "to the norm." Creative thinking is in a different category from "the way things are always done." Creative thinking encourages new ways of doing and thinking about things, and this leads to more experiences of living your dreams.

I recently went to the dentist to get my teeth cleaned. The hygienist explained that I was overdue for X-rays and that there were possible cavities to be discussed.

I felt immediately resistant to this news and then remembered that I had a choice about how to proceed. I explained that it felt overwhelming right then to hear more about my teeth and requested that she take the X-rays and I would come back later to discuss the results. She said, "Well, the

We can change our clocks and calendars to support ourselves and our dreams

dentist doesn't usually work like that, but I suppose we could." (Actually, she and the dentist have been exceedingly supportive of my unusual timetable, because they're a creative dental office!)

It might not be ideal, or the "best way" but it worked well for me.

Whatever works well for me gives me more time to live my creative dreams, even if it sometimes doesn't make sense to someone else.

REBELLING AND NONCONFORMING are free and easy to try. Many of us hesitate because of the fear of a bad response. If you rebel calmly and consciously, people usually have a good response, because the rebellion activates their creative thinking.

You might:

Buy food to bring to a potluck instead of making it.

React cheerfully when someone honks at you.

Ask the bank teller to make an exception.

Request that the seat on the plane be empty next to you, and explain that you'll welcome whoever sits there if this isn't possible.

We can practice rebellion and nonconformity in our daily lives in small ways. This will remind us that we can choose how we live, and that we can make creative choices. These creative choices will lead to more experiences of creative dream-living.

Guilt

As you experiment with doing things badly, rebelling, and nonconforming, you may encounter guilt. You might also feel guilty for having creative dreams!

The dictionary says that guilt is: The state or fact of having committed a crime, legal offense, or wrongdoing.

If you feel guilty for asking for what you'd like or need, or how you'd like to live your life, how have you defined guilt?

Guilt is incredibly unproductive, often

unnecessary, and most often not properly defined. It is unproductive because it can stop you from actively living your creative dream life.

Living your creative dreams might awaken you to feelings of guilt, and you can choose how to respond to guilty feelings. You can also explore the roots of guilt in your life and how you started believing that guilt was necessary or valuable. Guilt is necessary when it relates to crimes or wrongdoings; it is not a benefit for creative dream-living.

Here are some common "guilt beliefs" with my comments:

Belief: I can't spend time on my creative dreams when there are children starving.

> **Comment:** Your guilt does not feed those children. Your not living your creative dreams does not benefit them. Your creative thinking can contribute to those starving children. You can redirect guilt into positive ways of thinking and acting.

Belief: When I ask for my needs, I feel guilty that I've asked for too much.

> **Comment:** Is your guilt based on actual fact? Often our guilt is only a perception or thought and we can choose what we perceive or think. Guilt is inappropriate in this circumstance.

Belief: If I ask for help, or don't help others, I feel guilty. How can I not feel guilty?

> **Comment:** Trying not to feel guilty is impossible. Your feelings don't understand logic. Feel the guilt and then let it go; let guilt teach you. Ask questions of guilt, like, "How is feeling guilty serving me or someone else?"

Failure

YOUR CREATIVE DREAMS need places and times for practice, process, and progress. They also need space to fail and not be started. This book is my permission to you to feel supported and guided in the whole process of creative dream-living, not just the parts that are working.

So many books put an emphasis on progressing, succeeding, and "making it happen."

Making your creative dreams real is all about the real stuff of life. While you're building your creative dreams, the rest of life races on, demanding your energy and attention.

on and... on and... on and... on and... Life races on

Most of us can't step away from the real world for very long. We usually work with our creative dreams in snippets and segments and bits of time that float by and we snatch them. In order to live your creative dreams, you need to give yourself permission to not live them very well at all.

You need to give yourself permission to fail.

Failure has a bad reputation. We become obsessed with success and forget that many failures made up that success.

We endow success with an aura of goodness and try to downplay or hide failure as though it's shameful.

Being willing to fail means that you are fully engaged in the process of living.

Failure is also a matter of perception. Here are some of my "failures":

I failed to graduate from college

I succeeded in self-education as a result.

I failed to have a child.

I gave birth to many books and other creative offerings.

I failed to forgive my older brother.

I learned how painful it is not to forgive, and have now forgiven him.

See if you can identify "failures" in your life and what gifts they gave you.

Welcome failure and step out of any shame or residual guilt.

Let failure assist you in living your creative dreams, and practice failing to pay too much attention to failure!

Frustration

LIVING CREATIVE DREAMS is full of frustrating experiences. There will be countless detours, delays, and mistakes. Your response to frustration will either accelerate or magnify it, or decrease or minimize it.

You can choose how to respond to frustration and think creatively about it.

Frustration is often a habitual learned response, and often involves reacting in a dramatic way.

"What do you mean the price went up? I need to buy these materials at the same price or I can't finish my project! Oh just forget it, I'm not shopping here again!"

It is frustrating to encounter unexpected price increases. It would be easier if these things didn't happen.

What would be less frustrating (besides no price increase)?
To respond calmly and objectively in that situation:

"Oh, the price has always been _____. Can I speak with a manager?"

You might make a new arrangement, or obtain a discount on other supplies. You might look elsewhere, and leave your frustration after leaving the store.

Examine and explore any tendency to become frustrated and see what's underneath. Usually there is some fear of change or loss. If you can address that change or loss, and communicate calmly with your fear, the need or tendency to be frustrated will often disappear.

See if frustration is a habit for you. Sometimes we act frustrated because that's what we learned in our families or in relationships.

Choose a new way to relate to frustration, and accept and allow frustration to be part of your creative dream living. If you attempt to just stop doing it, you are likely to become frustrated!

Impatience

Making your creative dreams real can be a slow, uneven process. You might make lots of progress quickly and then find yourself in a long period of inactivity. Other parts of your life may claim your time and attention, and you might begin to feel impatient about your creative dream.

I have many experiences of impatience in my creative dream-living, and can say that it is both positive and negative. It is positive when it causes me to take action when I've been stuck. It is negative when it causes me to take action that isn't well thought out. Impatience often causes hasty choices and poorly timed actions.

Making your creative dreams real is part of living your creative dream life, and life requires **patience.**

If you practice impatience, you will create a climate that reinforces impatience. If you practice patience, the climate you create will support more patience.

Of course, as a person who most often practices impatience, I don't have as much experience with patience, but I can tell from a distance that it's true.

Being patient with our creative dreams, our lives, and ourselves can only shelter and nourish us. Being impatient tears those shelters down.

Most of my pain comes from some form of impatience. I am learning ways to be patient with myself and my creative dreams.

Impatience can become

Don't Work Harder

Working hard is highly overrated. We often misuse our energy trying just to "get things done." We forget about what creative dream-living needs.

Creative dream-living happens when we let our pace be easy and gentle. This is similar to "going with the flow." (Although that phrase awakens my resistant self and makes me want to struggle just to be opposite.) So how can we develop our capacity to "flow with the go"?

I think we do this when we recognize that the "flow" contains all of it: failure, guilt, frustration, impatience, and rebellion. When we can allow ourselves to contain these and other qualities fully, we can learn to use them to *start* the flow.

SOMETIMES PEOPLE READ MY BOOKS and see the bright colors and the little drawings and decide that I am this **whimsical, free, creative spirit** who just flows along from one adventure to another. I will tell you that I'm pretty tightly wound and prone to **crabby**, controlling outbursts.

I don't flow as much as seep, bubble, and rush.

The truth is, we are all in some opposition to "going with the flow."

We are all diverted, delayed, and altogether absent from the flow.

Creative dream-living means **finding your way back to that flow** over and over again no matter what kind of personality you have.

Nobody is just naturally "going with the flow" all the time, and this is perfectly fine. We can take who and how we are right now, and enter the flow at any time.

All of the difficult parts of creative dream-living contribute to us. How you live with those difficulties is your creative choice.

Ecstatic Eighth Month

Living Your Creative Dreams

☆

week one

A Game or Something to Try

Form a Grudge Group

This can consist of just you and one other friend.

Agree that whatever is shared is not to be repeated to others.

Set a timer and for 10 to 15 minutes each person states all the reasons or grudges that get in the way of his or her creative dream-living. This is a good outlet for judgments and blame.

As one person speaks, the other person takes notes.

At the end of the 30 minutes, the grudges and notes are gathered for burning or recycling.

Create a closing statement. For example, "I am no longer blocked or stopped by any person or reason. I gladly let these grudges go."

☆

week two

A GIFT for You

I SEND YOU . . .
A scoop of stars and a cloak of patience.

You can carry the scoop of stars wherever you go, to illuminate your path.

Knowing that you're glowing will help you if you get scared or lost.

Your cloak of patience is lightweight and invisible to anyone else. It folds up to the size of a penny, and you can put it on any time to magnify your experiences of patience. Eventually, you absorb the cloak into your body and patience becomes an intrinsic part of you.

☆

week three

A Positive Challenge (I Dare You)

Make a procrastination list

Use your creative dream guidebook or blank paper.

Write down things that you typically postpone longer than you'd like.

You could start with,

"I procrastinate about: _____

_____

_____

_____

_____."

You already know these things, but writing them down gets them out of your head and speeds up your creativity receptivity.

If you're not a procrastinator, offer to support someone who is, by assisting him or her in making this list.

RADIANT Resources

week four

When You're Falling, Dive
   Cheri Huber

The Places That Scare You: A Guide to
Fearlessness in Difficult Times
   Pema Chödrön

Transformation Soup: Healing for the Splendidly Imperfect
   SARK

The Power of Patience: How to Slow the Rush and Enjoy More
Happiness, Success and Peace of Mind Everyday
   M. J. Ryan

Healing Through the Dark Emotions: The Wisdom of Grief,
Fear and Despair
   Miriam Greenspan

I Thought We'd Never Speak Again: The Road from
Estrangement to Reconciliation
   Laura Davis

I Know Why the Caged Bird Sings
   Maya Angelou

Radical Acceptance: Embracing Your Life with the Heart of a Buddha
   Tara Brach, Ph.D.

Change Your Brain, Change Your Life: A Breakthrough Program
for Conquering Anxiety, Depression, Obsessiveness,
Anger and Impulsiveness
   Daniel G. Amen, M.D.

Life Makeovers: 52 Practical and Inspiring Ways to Improve Your Life One Week at a Time
    Cheryl Richardson

The Complete Collected Poems of Maya Angelou

Stand Still Like the Hummingbird
    Henry Miller

www.thesunmagazine.com
www.healingenvironments.org
www.kerismith.com

CHAPTER NINE

Nourishing
Ninth Month

Nourishing You and Your Creative Dreams

The purpose of this chapter is to refresh you and your creative dreams, and to assist you if you feel stuck.

What Feels Nourishing?

SOMETIMES WHEN I AM FOCUSED on a creative dream or project, I can forget to nourish myself. I can also forget to nourish myself if I am procrastinating, avoiding, or hiding from focusing on a creative dream. Either too much activity or not enough can feel draining or exhausting. It can be tricky to identify the type of nourishment that I need.

I've learned to keep notes about **what inspires or nourishes me** so I can refer to them when I feel drained or depleted. If I try to remember what feels nourishing when I am already depleted, I will probably find myself choosing the wrong nourishment. I might find myself:

Eating my emotions.

Sleeping when not tired.

Being alone when I really need company.

The right nourishment fills us up from the inside. It gives us:

Surprise and curiosity.

Adventure and pleasure.

Willingness to go inside.

The ability to ask and receive.

If I am curious and seeking new experiences, I can probably surprise myself in some way, which leads to brand-new experiences.

HAVING ADVENTURES on a regular basis leads to habits of pleasure.

Being willing to go inside myself and discover what's there, can lead to a fresh perspective and new ideas.

Every time I can ask for and receive comfort, care, attention, and assistance, I can expand my capacity to extend this to others.

We don't automatically nourish ourselves.

We're not often taught to nourish ourselves when we're young. Our ability to self-nourish can be studied, practiced, and expanded upon. This nourishment is necessary in order to make creative dreams real.

If we are well nourished, our creative dreams will leap out to play and be seen. Our self-nourishment will literally feed our creative dreams. Creative dreams need light and oxygen in order to grow.

Here are some notes from my journals on the subject of self-nourishment:

1. Waking up feeling lonely and off-balance

What do I need to look at?
Nutrition check (what have I been eating?)

"All That we see or seem is But A dream within A dream"
e dgar Allan poe

Relationship to gratitude (what am I receiving?)

Reaching out (who can be replenished?)

2. Feeling overwhelmed

   What do I need?

   What takes the pressure off? (things to let go of)

   What to disengage from? (appropriate uses of the word no)

   Balance check (how I am eating/sleeping/loving/working)

Nourishment Experiences and Examples

NOURISHMENT sometimes means doing the opposite of what you would usually do. Recently, I felt overwhelmed and pressured by my work, and called my friend Larry for some friendly conversation and diversion.

Larry suddenly declared, "It's time you came over, saw my new office, and went out to dinner with me."

Usually I would want to discuss and control all the particulars, time, etc. Instead I just said, "O.K., see you soon" and hung up the phone. I felt a surge of energy and enthusiasm, and a lifting of feeling pressured and overwhelmed. Larry commented on how nice it was to simply hear my agreement to a plan he proposed.

The evening felt nourishing in a way that I hadn't planned or controlled, and I intend to be open to more surprising and nourishing encounters.

Nourishment can come in forms and ways we don't expect:

My friend Sabrina invited me to a party at her new art studio, and I dearly wanted to go. On the day before the party, I felt overworked and like I might be getting sick, so I called Sabrina and left a message intending to just let her know that I might not be attending. Instead, I started crying on the voice mail and recounting how bad I was feeling. I then said, "Be disappointed if you need to, but please call me with some support if you can."

She called with this message:

"This is the angel of health, understanding, and empathy. I send you a sweet breeze that smells of lavender, a candle that burns through indigo glass, a book that opens to the perfect page about letting go, a fig tree out your window, a few narcissus, and a tiny little book made by a friend."

I felt so loved and restored when I heard this message, and was able to attend the party, which filled me with sunshine, bing cherries, deep conversations, and gazing at the sunset.

I returned to my work feeling rejuvenated and full of energy.

We can also practice self-nourishment when the story doesn't go this way:

When a friend *is* disappointed and says so.

When someone is counting on us and we can't deliver.

When our friend leaves a crabby message.

This is why we go inside for our nourishment before we go outside. Then we will not lose our feelings of nourishment based on somebody's reaction or feelings.

This is one of our most important assignments as creative dream-livers.

PRACTICE NOURISHING YOURSELF FIRST. This takes focus and concentration because most of us are used to searching for nourishment from outside sources.

Learn what feels truly nourishing to you and

keep notes for future reference. People can nourish us just by their existence. When we read or hear about other people living their creative dreams it can nourish or refresh our dreams.

I asked my friend Maggie to share her nourishing creative dream of adopting a child:

> *As I write this, my husband and I are thick in the middle of the paperwork required to adopt our daughter from another country. But, even though we're pretty sure she hasn't even been born yet—and maybe not even been conceived yet—she is very real to me. She has already appeared in my dreams; I dreamt that a woman at the orphanage was telling me that they had been deciding between two babies to join our family, and that this was the one they had chosen—when they put her in my arms, I loved her instantaneously, with a deep, abiding, and immediate love!*
>
> *So my new "creative dream" has quite literally visited me in my dreams, and in waking hours I feel as if I am living the life of my dreams. My child is on her way to us; I am married to a partner I love and admire; I live in a house I feel daily gratitude for, in the city that still takes my breath away. I have been blessed with the opportunity to write*

books on the topics that I find the most meaningful personally (spiritual life and practice); and I have created a coaching business called The New Story that allows me to support others in creating their life dreams. What inspires me the most about creative dreams is that they are themselves generative. Each dream I have ever fulfilled (or which God has graced me with) has been a part of another; they are all pieces of the colorful, sometimes well-planned, sometimes raggedy, quilt that is my life.

And in that sense, I do believe that living out our creative dreams helps the world. When we demonstrate the possibilities for our lives, when we live into our dreams, our examples can inspire others. To continue with the quilt analogy, we all have "patches" in our lives that are dark and torn. Sometimes, what can keep us going is to see through another's life that dreams can come true—that anything truly is possible. When we share our stories of achievement purposefully, with the intention of encouraging another, we help to supply the fuel of hope. Sometimes, just knowing that someone else has done something we really want to do can be the catalyst that moves our creative dreams forward.

Here's an example: In the nearly nineties, I was unwillingly single, unenthusiastically living in the Midwest, and unhappily employed. During a trip to Seattle, I wandered into a bookstore and happened to pick up a colorful volume called A Creative Companion by someone named SARK. I read the whole thing in one sitting, delighting in the stories told by this wonderful woman who was living one of my dreams—being an author—in the city I wanted to be doing it in (San Francisco). At the time, those possibilities seemed far,

far away. Just a decade or so later, I live in that same city, have four published books of my own, am joyfully married, and count as one of the many blessings of my life the fact that Susan Ariel Rainbow Kennedy has become a beloved friend. Possibilities abound, miracles happen. Creative dreams do come true—believe it!

I am nourished and inspired by Maggie's life and story. We are surrounded by nourishment opportunities and forget to look for them!

Ordinary Days as Dream Nourishment

WE CAN TAKE OUR "ORDINARY" DAYS and turn them into ways to refresh and nourish our creative dreams. Part of this is learning to see whatever we do and are, as contributors to creative dream-living. We tend to think that we need to live unusual lives in exotic locations in order to be "really" living our creative dreams. All of our tiny dream moments contribute to our creative dream-living.

Two women from Canada called my inspiration line and left a message for me with just the sound of their 2 kids playing in the bathtub. Those giggling, chortling, splashing sounds have been nourishing my spirit for weeks.

THe MUsic in THe BATH TUB

My friend Joshua calls and leaves quotes by the poet Rumi on my voice mail. He then began reading a series of letters by the author Henry Miller. These words have nourished my soul.

It is also important to be nourished by the parts of our ordinary days that don't work very well. I am often struck by how messy and inconvenient it is to be human.

I continually forget that challenges are an intrinsic part of feeling nourished. It is by challenges that we learn what doesn't feel nourishing, and that we can return over and over again to feeling nourished.

Give yourself permission to turn the icky, crabby, unwelcome parts of your ordinary days into a particular kind of nourishment. We need all the flavors and textures in order to be truly nourished—not just the sweet, simple, glowing things. I'm frequently surprised to discover the gifts that were hidden in a "bad day": realizations and discoveries I might not have made without particular kinds of challenges.

Another important ingredient for nourishment is delight. Find out what delights you, because your answers hold clues to living more of your creative dreams.

I am delighted by:

the unexpected
the unusual in the ordinary
meaningful encounters with "strangers"

I am inspired and nourished by spontaneous encounters with strangers. People often ask me if I'm friends with someone in a store or a restaurant because I often speak in familiar, curious tones with people I don't know.

I do not always do this! Sometimes I am feeling crabby, introverted, or just hiding out in some way

I often wonder why we act so afraid of each other. I think that we forget how similar we are to each other. I know that we forget how exquisite we are.

Remember that people you don't know are filled with delights and wonders that could nourish and inspire you. All you need to do is connect with them in some way.

How's Your Creative Dream?

Are you:

Thinking about it?

If you're thinking about your creative dream, what have you been thinking about? Can you make some notes or tape record thoughts so your dream can get out of your head? Or does it need to stay at the thinking stage? How long do you need to be in the thinking stage?

Exploring?

If you've been exploring the subject of your creative dream, what have you discovered? Can you express this in some way?

Doing things?

What things are you doing? Can you make a list?

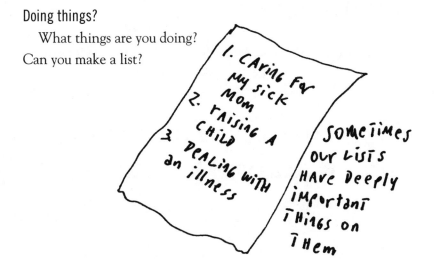

1. CARing For My sick Mom
2. rAising A CHILD
3. DEALing with an illness

Sometimes our Lists HAve Deeply important Things on THem

Avoiding?

If you've been avoiding, what have you been doing or feeling while avoiding? Can you describe some things?

Hiding?

What's happened in the hiding time? Can you share or list your experiences?

Quitting?

If you're quitting, can you describe what quitting will bring you and how or why you decided to quit?

Starting over?

Can you detail what this means to you?

Revising?

What needed revision and how will revising be of benefit?

Inventing?

What kinds of inventing have you been doing?

These questions are meant to give you the opportunity to make your creative dream experiences real, and to let them out of your head and into the physical world.

One of the least nourishing experiences about creative dreams is feeling stuck. When we get stuck, nourishment can set us free, but first we need to explore "stuckness."

What If You're Stuck with Your Creative Dream(s)?

WHAT IS YOUR DEFINITION OF BEING STUCK? If being stuck is by definition a lack of movement or activity, how long has this been the case?

If you've been stuck longer than one year, go back to the Land of No (chapter 2) and reread.

If you've been stuck less than a year, let's unravel your "stuckness" through a series of questions:

1. Have you reached a certain point with your creative dream and are not sure what to do next?

Try:

> Creative dream starters on page 245
>
> Question-and-answer section on page 246
>
> Rereading the World of Yes on page 67
>
> Consulting www.planetsark.com

2. Are you overwhelmed, tired, overworked, or just "out of enthusiasm" for your creative dream?

Try:

> Quitting or taking a break
>
> Resting or napping more than usual
>
> Creative dream starters on page 245
>
> Asking a friend for support in a new way

3. Did you try a number of things that didn't work and are discouraged with your progress?

Try:

> MicroMOVEment chapter on page 88
>
> Support systems chapter on page 105
>
> Dream stoppers section on page 244

Are you truly "stuck" or just temporarily stopped? Usually being stuck is a state of mind that responds to some kind of change.

4. When was the last time you did something new with regard to your creative dream? What was it?

Try:

World of Yes on page 67

Creative dream questions on page 163

Questions and answers on page 246

Defend your description of being stuck. Write about it in your creative dream guidebook in detail. List the ways you feel stuck and exactly what being stuck feels like.

Now ask your wise self to write a way out of stuckness. Respond to each thing you've written or listed in an opposite way.

It also helps in the nourishment of dreams to explore your particular style of dreaming.

Style and Pace of Dreams
What Is the Pace of Your Dream(s)?

Fast-moving creative dreams:

Zip along

Happen swiftly

Gain energy quickly

Things occur seemingly without effort

People and things appear just when needed

Slow-moving dreams:

Happen in bits and pieces

Have periods of silence and inactivity

Seem to be forgotten

Things happen in slow motion

Lots of thinking and deliberation

Some types of creative dreams will have elements of both fast and slow movements. You can learn how to nourish yourself and your dreams by exploring how you like to move with your dreams.

It is important not to assign goodness to the fast-moving pace, and discouragement to the slow-moving pace.

If your natural pace seems to be fast-moving, are you assisting others with their creative dreams, either through mentoring or teaching?

If your pace seems to be slow-moving, how are you doing with acceptance of yourself? Are you participating in support systems?

Making creative dreams real involves learning about your style and pace, and not closing down or becoming isolated in response to your process of movement. Our culture is focused on success, progress, and accomplishment without enough honoring of the process that gets us there.

We must honor that process.

This honoring involves refusing to compare yourself with anyone. This is a difficult assignment and can only occur with time and conscious practice. Becoming aware of the desire to compare is a good place to begin.

If you are already actively comparing, make an ongoing list of your comparisons and let your wise self respond. Refer to this list whenever comparisons appear.

What Do You and Your Creative Dreams Need?

The care and nourishment of creative dreams involves taking care of the dreamer as well as the dreams.

Are you practicing self-care? Page 112

Does your creative dream need:

Refreshment?

Something new, fresh, or interesting.

Movement?

Physically changing the environment or something about the creative dream.

Nurturing?

Some kind of shelter or resting place.

Do you need:

Adventure?

Interacting with the world in a fresh way.

Re invention?

Taking the invention of yourself and revising it in some tiny or large way.

Attitude revision?

Examining your attitude for "Land of No" qualities. Experiment with shifting your attitude.

In order to make space in your life for more of your creative dreams, you might need to make changes and adjust some of your habits and routines.

I tend to cling to most things, and generally abhor changing my habits. At the same time, I know that my creative dreams are nourished by new behaviors and experiences. I received great benefit from something the author Cheryl Richardson said: "Don't try to wedge new behaviors into an already too full schedule. Take something out of that schedule."

Of course at first I thought there was nothing I could remove from my schedule, until I looked more closely and saw that I could make adjustments to my television watching and telephone talking times. I made some simple changes, and found space and time for more of my creative dreams.

Sometimes what I need isn't the same as what I want, and I'm continually learning new things about what I and my creative dreams need and what is most nourishing.

Nourishing Ninth Month

Nourishing You and Your Creative Dreams

☆

week one

A Game or Something to Try

Call a few friends and ask them to participate in your creative dream development project. If you have a creative dream, share it with them.

Ask the following questions:

Can you imagine me living even more of my creative dream?

What would that look like?

In what ways do you see me already living my dream?

Take notes about what they say, make lists, and ask them not to ask you about this again until you request it. (It's easy to begin imagining that your friends are pressuring you in some way.) As your dreams develop, you might choose to share specific details with these same friends.

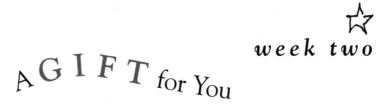

week two

A GIFT for You

I SEND YOU ...

A winding path that leads to a gate, which leads to the sea. You arrive to find a tea party all set up, and you're the first guest to arrive. You look closely at the table, and there are name tags for all your "inside children" at all of their various ages. There is a tiny cradle, a high chair, a hammock, and big comfortable stuffed chairs.

Surrounded by lavender and napping deeply

You feel profoundly rested and refreshed by this vision, and notice that there is no sense of time, or urgency, or anything at all to do. You realize that this expansive state is your natural birthright, and you lie down in the soft cloth hammock that is surrounded by lavender, and fall into a deep, helpless nap.

week three
A Positive Challenge (I Dare You)

Imagine that your creative dream is in full bloom.
Write a detailed description of you living this dream.
What does it look, feel, smell, sound like?

Be as expansive and descriptive as possible:

Where and how are you living?

What are you doing?

Who is there?

week four
RADIANT Resources

Change Your Life without Getting Out of Bed
  SARK

Quirkyalone: A Manifesto for Uncompromising Romantics
  Sasha Cagen

The Mind-Body Makeover Project: A 12-Week Plan for Transforming Your Body and Your Life
  Michael Gerrish and Cheryl Richardson

Brave on the Rocks: If You Don't Go, You Don't See
  Sabrina Ward Harrison

When Things Fall Apart: Heart Advice for Difficult Times
  Pema Chödrön

You Don't Have to Write a Book!
  Sidra Stone and Hal Stone

The Nine Modern Day Muses: 10 Guides to Creative Inspiration for Artists, Poets, Lovers, and Other Mortals Wanting to Live a Dazzling Existence
  Jill Badonsky

Stillness Speaks
  Eckhart Tolle

www.karendrucker.com
www.absolutewrite.com
www.eckharttolle.com
www.wendy.com/letterwriting
www.quirkyalone.net/qa/

CHAPTER TEN

Terrific
Tenth Month

What You and Your Dreams Need Now

The purpose of this chapter is to discover what stage your dream is at and where it needs to go or grow.

Where Does Your Creative Dream Need to Go or Grow?

YOU ARE THE CHANNEL and vehicle for your creative dreams. Every creative dream needs a human channel to bring it into existence and make it real.

What kind of channel or vehicle are you?

Keeping the channel open is your most important job. Often we clog our channels with worry, anxiety, stress, or negativity. Then we're so "busy" dealing with those states, we have no time or energy to create anything new.

Being a good vehicle is another very important part of making dreams real. The vehicle operates the dream and moves it from one place to another. Many of us keep our dream vehicle in the garage with the door locked.

In order to find out what your creative dream needs, you need to be able to:

Describe where your dream is currently

The actuality of it, not where you wish it was

Let your dream educate and inform you

You do this by literally asking your dream what it needs from you now

Move from one level to another with your dream

You do this by stating what it would take to move to the next level, and describe that level

In order to give your dream what it needs, you need to be:

Willing

Curious

Flexible

Committed

Patient

Determined

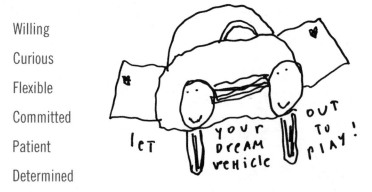

let your dream vehicle OUT TO PLAY!

You also need to be able to explore the opposites of each of these qualities.

Stages of Dream Development

It is helpful to uncover which stage your dream is at in order to find out where it needs to go next.

See if you can determine which of those stages your dream or dreams are at. It is common to have more than one dream, at different stages. Some dreams stay at the "egg" stage for many years. Some dreams never become "adult." Whatever stage your creative dream is at, it is important to find out what you and your dream need along the way and create a system of support while you make your creative dream real.

1. AT THE EGG STAGE (idea, beginning, tiny thought), in order to make your creative dream real, you will need:

Nourishment (inner and outer)

Listening (from yourself and others)

Cradling/shelter (safety)

Patience (for the growing)

MicroMOVEments (for movement and completion)

2. AT THE HATCHED STAGE (idea born, made visible, tangible, physical) you will need:

Supporters/cheerleaders (to encourage your dream and you)

Compassionate witnesses (to just listen)

Celebrations (to acknowledge growth)

MicroMOVEments (movement and completion)

3. AT THE INFANT STAGE (born and developing), you will need:

Healthy routines (for you and your creative dream)

Assistance (from other people or systems)

Acknowledgement (from yourself and others)

MicroMOVEments (movement and completion)

"To Allow oneself To Be carried Away By A Multitude of Conflicting Concerns, To Consider Too Many Demands, To Commit oneself To too Many projects, To Want To Help in everything is To succumb To violence. The Frenzy of The Activist neutralizes His or Her Work for peace"   Thomas Merton

4. AT THE TODDLER STAGE (growing and dependent) you will need:

> More assistance (for when you aren't there)
>
> Increased self-care (for yourself)
>
> Community involvement (to circumvent isolation)
>
> MicroMOVEments (movement and completion)

5. AT THE CHILD STAGE (growing quickly, shifting dependency) you will need:

> Allowing independence (test your creative dream in the world)
>
> Practicing new skills (asking for unfamiliar things for your creative dream)
>
> Sharing tasks (accepting help/receiving)
>
> MicroMOVEments (movement and completion)

6. AT THE ADOLESCENT STAGE (grown, becoming interdependent) you will need:

> Less rigid guidelines (experimenting with types and styles of growth)
>
> Intuitive guidance (letting your "belly brain" decide)
>
> Healthy separation (allowing your creative dream to be separate from you)
>
> Conflict resolution (handling things that don't work)

7. AT THE ADULT STAGE (all grown up, interdependent, integrated) you will need:

> Release of attendance (ceasing supervision on a consistent basis)
>
> Launching/letting go (releasing control)
>
> Acceptance of loss and change (as your creative dream grows up, you will feel loss)
>
> Introduction of new creative dreams (as dreams grow, replace them with your new ones)

THESE STAGES of dream development are not meant to be followed in a linear fashion. It is not "better" to have adult dreams. Some dreams stay in earlier stages of development for their entire existence.

I challenge you not to "make progress" with your creative dream, but to "make process." This means that the outcome is not the point.

MAKiNG
PrOcess
is More
of an adventure

Making your creative dream real is a choice, and you might also choose *not* to do that. Some dreams never become real, and these kinds are also nourishing.

Having an active creative dream life does not necessitate "going public" or "making it real." You might be a private dream-liver who chooses to think and/or talk about your creative dreams and not take any action. This causes changes just by the energy of those thoughts. Ask yourself the following:

Am I actually a private dream-liver or am I hiding there to avoid making my dreams real?

You will know the answer.

It is not necessary to make money or be known for your creative dream to have value. Perhaps you have a creative dream to help children in Zimbabwe or East Los Angeles. Maybe you will never be recognized or acknowledged for work you do.

This does not diminish the effect of your creative dream. For writers, being published does not make the words glow brighter. The point of creative dreams is not to "go public" or make money, but to make those dreams real in your life.

Having a child is a private creative dream that manifests in a human bean who can affect the whole world with his or her creative dreams.

Making creative dreams real can be public or private. Each has equal yet different value.

dedicated to MY DEAR BroTHer andrew and His Hi

YOUR CREATIVE DREAMS WILL CALL FOR WHAT THEY NEED, and find their place in our world. You can trust that the living of your creative dreams is far more important than any type of outcome.

How can your creative dream life continue to grow even if you're not "working on it?"

Progress is measured by existence as well as by activity. If your creative dream exists, it is real and alive. **Activity is not the only measure.**

How Do Dreams Get to Where They Need to Go?

CREATIVE DREAMS HAVE their own energy and momentum and can lead or propel you to do things you wouldn't ordinarily do for yourself personally. I've made requests for my creative dreams that I would be far too shy to make without my creative dream.

Is there somewhere your creative dream needs to go and you're the one stopping it?

We stop dreams by:

Hiding

"I have a lot of amazing _____,but I just never take them out."

Minimizing

"Oh, I used to dream about doing _____,but it's too late now and I probably wouldn't be any good."

Substituting

"I had a dream once about being _____, but it's better that I just went ahead and did _____ instead."

every Human Bean is A Dreamer

Dreams cannot get to where they need to go without your participation and involvement.

This might mean:

Being uncomfortable

Dreams sometimes require new or unfamiliar behaviors

Sharing your dream

Sometimes we need other people to be involved

Leaving what feels safe

Leaps of faith are sometimes necessary

Creative dreams might move differently than you thought.

You might be ready to leap and look back to see your dream crawling.

Your dream might leap, and you might be tiptoeing behind, or right alongside.

Your dream may need you to lead or follow, to get where it needs to go.

How this happens is by your keen attention, insatiable interest, and continual involvement.

Assessing and Reassessing Your Creative Dream

SOMETIMES IN ORDER to know where your creative dream needs to go or grow, you will need to assess its effect and value in your life.

My younger brother Andrew dreamed of teaching, and then fulfilled that dream for three years. He purposely chose to teach at a school with very little money, and at one point was teaching geography without a map. He then had his students create maps. His teaching dream changed shape with time and challenges, and he reassessed and realized that he needed to take a break from teaching and explore a different dream. One of his new dreams is to hike the Pacific Crest Trail from Mexico to Canada.

I believe that we are meant to try and explore as many dreams as we wish. It might be tempting to think that if you're educated for something, you better stay in it and "make it worthwhile."

But it is even more important to assess how worthwhile your dream is while you're actually living it.

Dreams can be much more appealing from a distance, or because of a lack of knowledge or experience.

In order to assess your dream, you need to be able to:

Allow yourself to see and feel how it is actually functioning

Create an objective way to assess how it functions

Ask for feedback from your team or support system

Wonder what you might dream next

Sometimes dreams change shape in the middle and lead us to new dreams that we would never have seen otherwise.

Another type of dream assessment is to see whether your dream is a:

Primary or core dream

This is usually one you've had for a long time; there can be more than one primary dream

Secondary or smaller dream

This is often an offshoot of a primary dream

You might choose to experience a collection of secondary dreams before exploring a primary dream.

For example, I believe that one of my primary dreams is to inspire others. One of my secondary dreams is to have a gallery show of art, letters, and eccentric tidbits.

i envision letters, paintings,
stacks of journals piled
high... All leading to
more creative connection

I continually assess which kind of dream I am living, and how it is serving me or others. I then reassess how it is going as I am having more experiences with it. I'm often surprised by dreams that I assess to be fulfilling or necessary, and then find in the reassessment that the timing is off, or my energy has shifted or changed.

I am convinced that **we need even more permission and freedom** to explore many dreams. We can utilize an assessment and reassessment process to help decide where a particular dream needs to go or grow.

Examples of Creative Dreams Growing

WE CAN CLEAR our creative channels and be available to dream new creative dreams and find ways to make them real.

I asked for people to share their creative dreams with me, and here are just three of the many that I received:

Dearest Susan,

I meant every word when I told you that you are truly a "good little vessel from God." I believe that you are channeling creative words and dreams to inspire each and every one of us.

As you may know, I am currently working on a creative dream. My creative dream involves the birthing of a "working ranch." This working ranch will be a place for women to take time out from the daily grind in an environment where they can foster their creative, authentic souls.

So often, we are hidden under the layers of lives that we have led. Our authentic selves just need a place where they are safe to explore and play. This is why I am creating a tax-exempt organization in order to make the dream a reality.

FROM SPARROW

When you're a vessel from God, you don't even need a boat!

Dearest SARK,

I would like to answer your request to hear our dreams and desires. When I was 20, I moved to the magical fairy-book town of Sighisoara, Romania, for a year to work with street children, orphans, and children with AIDS. Here I was walking along cobblestone streets with flower boxes in every window . . . sipping peach nectar by moonlight in a small café. But, with all the beauty that was surrounding me in this cozy little town, I was still facing the amazing pain of working with these children who were hurting and needed so much love. I could feel all of my insides going gray and muted and it was at that time that your books spoke to me and helped me to investigate my pain. It is now seven years later and my biggest dream and desire is to go back there and create a center where the street children can come for soup made with love and create a place where they can cry, paint, laugh, receive hugs, and curl up on soft pillows with books. That is my dream.

FROM AMY DARE

My creative dream is to research and write about resistance movements in World War II. I want to meet with people who were in the movements and find out what their "last straws" were: what happened that made them realize that the only way to change the world was if they did it themselves. I think these are such amazing stories of courage and selflessness. They truly gave the gift of life to many people who had been destined to die. Thanks for making me write it down! It makes it feel much more real and attainable just to share it with the anonymous masses. :)

FROM: DE

Quitting and Postponing Dreams

PART OF THE ASSESSMENT and reassessment process involves making creative dream decisions.

As the channel and vehicle for your creative dream, you are the best qualified to do this. We are not encouraged or supported in quitting as much as we are for "keeping trying."

Some dreams need to end.

You can explore this by:

Making an "I quit" statement about your creative dream and list the reasons.

See if you feel relief. If you do, it may be time to quit that particular dream.

You might feel sadness, anxiety, or worry about quitting your dream. This is natural, and might mean that you need to reassess your decision to quit. Some dreams are not meant to end, but to rest for a while.

Postponing dreams is a good way to let them rest. In the meantime, you can explore and discover what you might need to reenergize that creative dream. Postponing also gives you time to replenish yourself and possibly recommit to your dream.

Making the decision to quit or postpone a dream takes the dream out of the active mode. This frees you to also consider other dreams, or maybe a part of that dream.

When I decided to restructure my company, it ended a dream I had to work with partners. As the company continued, I found that working alone with a virtual assistant and freelance people was more rewarding for me and my way of doing business. My former partners are also now engaged in new creative dreams. I wrote a book in 1980 that never got published, so I postponed that particular dream until 1989 when I published my first book.

See if you can describe dreams that you've quit or postponed, and what happened as a result.

Dreams That Lead the Way

Some creative dreams have the kind of power and energy that ask you to follow along. You'll notice this by:

Serendipity: The faculty of making fortunate discoveries by accident

Synchronicity: Meaningful coincidences

You might also feel deeply moved to attend to or birth your dream. This might cause you to:

Learn new skills

Invent new systems

Collaborate or cocreate

Face old fears

When I wrote *Succulent Wild Woman* in 1997, it fulfilled a powerful dream I had to help empower women *and men* to think differently about women in the world. This dream led the way after I saw, etched into the cement on a San Francisco sidewalk, the words:

I DECIDED THAT IT WAS TIME
to reveal my power as a succulent wild woman and inspire others to do the same. That book became a best seller and led the way for other books to follow.

I had a very strong sense that this dream was leading me, and made a decision to follow it like a strong current in the water. I tuned up my vehicle and adjusted my channel, because both needed revising for this new dream.

I believe that we need to keep asking the question,

What kind of vehicle and channel am I for my creative dream? And revise it if needed.

A creative dream that leads the way will inspire you to be the best channel and vehicle possible. Be willing to make changes in yourself if your dream calls for it.

Examples of Creative Dreams That Grew

NEAR MY HOME IN SAN FRANCISCO are the results of many creative dreams. Here are just a few of my favorites:

☆ A lush, tumbling garden in the city started by one woman with a creative dream. The garden grew larger along with her creative dream, and developers wanted to use the land for buildings. This woman and her friends organized and sold square inches of this garden for $10 an inch, and raised enough money to buy the land and keep it as a garden forever.

☆ An eleven-year-old boy used to visit the garden and dream of tending it. Thirty years later, he is now the gardener, living his creative dream in a small house right near the hydrangea bushes.

☆ A man dreamed of a city park in a steep, small piece of land near his home. He drew up plans, raised the money, and halved railroad ties for steps. It is now the tiniest city park in San Francisco.

☆ A corner store that had a hundred-year-old history was to be closed forever because the owners were retiring and a new deal with the landlords couldn't be worked out. One man with the dream of owning and operating it negotiated a new deal after everyone said it was hopeless, and the store is thriving today.

Our creative dreams have power and purpose, and they are all around you, all the time. Creative dreams often start in an "impossible situation," and one of the most impossible was the Del Coronado Hotel in San Diego, California.

In the late 1800s, two men had the creative dream of building a fabulous hotel. They had no money or experience, but they had their creative vision. They drew pictures of their hotel, and began

Hotel Del Coronado - San Diego

acting as if they knew what they were doing. They floated redwood logs down from San Francisco, which they had bartered for, and hired teams of workers, whom they paid with promises of partial ownership. They attracted the attention of Thomas Edison, who put lights in the hotel (the first electricity in a commercial building), and L. Frank Baum (author of *The Wonderful Wizard of Oz*), who designed much of the architecture. In three months their creative dreams had built this hotel!

When I heard those stories of the building of that hotel, I felt incredibly energized and full of creative energy. I believe that creative dreams are our most power-full energy source.

Even when we are not actively living our creative dreams, we can benefit and be of benefit to other creative dreams and dreamers. We are each affected by the energy of creative dreams.

Creative dreams do not need to be only large or successful to contribute to our world. There are millions of miniature creative dreams and creative actions going on every day.

Every act of kindness comes from a creatively dreaming heart.

We underestimate our contribution if we measure only creative dreams made real. We must also measure all the steps along the way toward becoming real. Having creative dreams and thinking about and discussing them has power too. We can activate creative dreams with our words and thoughts.

To be actively engaged in creatively dreaming is part of our purpose as human beings. Making those creative dreams real and physical in our world is another part, and it is a privilege. The power of people making their creative dreams real is breathtaking. Our creative dreams can solve or affect every challenge we face.

Your creative dreams have this power. It can be scary to activate this kind of power if you've forgotten who you are and what your purpose is. We all forget this, and then we are reminded —by a book, or a film, or someone else's creative dream. This reminding happens over and over again.

Let others' dream stories activate you! ✦

Hi SARK,

Your unabashed embracing of creativity is soooo refreshing.

My dream is that everyone on the planet gains the psychological tools to reach a state of unreserved allowing of life's lusciousness.

Thanks for the delight,

Julie

Terrific Tenth Month

What You and Your Dreams Need Now

☆
week one

A Game or Something to Try

Create an Acknowledgement Poster

Put up a big white piece of paper. List and describe every action taken or miracle associated with your creative dream. Each time something happens positively about your creative dream, make a note of it and add it to this poster. This will encourage even more good things to happen.

We often forget what has already happened, who has helped us, and what tiny miracles assisted us along the way. This kind of poster honors and acknowledges those steps. This also means that you will be more aware of what you're creating and accomplishing.

☆
week two

A G I F T for You

I SEND YOU . . .

A sweet nap at the bottom of a sun-warmed canoe. Someone else is paddling, and there is a soft thunk as the paddle touches the side of the canoe. You are smiling slightly and admiring the sky. Water splashes up periodically, and you lie in a state of timeless wonder. You are going somewhere, but it doesn't matter when you get there. Your body feels light and strong and flexible. Take a deep breath and another. You are in a state of awakened vulnerability. All is well.

You lie in a state of timeless wonder

week three
A Positive Challenge (I Dare You)

Ask a friend or Creative Dream Team member to help you with one of your creative dreams.

In your Creative Dream Guidebook, or on blank paper, list these questions and your answers:

My creative dream is currently _____.

I wish my dream was _____.

3 things that would really help me right now are:

    1. _____

    2. _____

    3. _____

I would like to brainstorm solutions and microMOVEments for those 3 things. Could you please help?

    1. _____

    2. _____

    3. _____

Help me to choose a date to meet with you again on my progress with these three things.

    We'll talk or get together by _____.

RADIANT Resources
week four

Ten Poems to Change Your Life
    Roger Housden

The Invitation
    Oriah Mountain Dreamer

The Vein of Gold: Journey to Your Creative Heart
    Julia Cameron

Living Juicy: Daily Morsels for Your Creative Soul
    SARK

What Should I Do With My Life? The True Story of People Who Answered the Ultimate Question
  Po Bronson

Living Out Loud: Activities to Fuel a Creative Life
  Keri Smith

Plant Your Dreams and the Miracles Will Grow
  Christine Miller

Living Your Joy
  Suzanne Falter-Barns

www.howmuchjoy.com
www.putumayo.com
www.raymonddavi.com
www.moonlight-chronicles.com

CHAPTER ELEVEN

Energizing Eleventh Month

Managing and Growing Your Creative Dreams

The purpose of this chapter is to learn about management and growth of your creative dreams.

Managing Your Dream

ONE OF THE MOST POWER-FULL THINGS I've learned about growing creative dreams is that **growth requires management.** This especially applies if you plan on making your creative dream public or bringing it to the marketplace.

I was mentored in this process by a business coach, reading books, and experimenting with my dreams. Through my experiences, I learned valuable lessons about how management relates to growth.

The manager part of you is different from the creative worker part of you. The creative worker only knows how to physically work directly on the creative dream. It's the part that sews or paints or makes phone calls, or physically does something.

The manager part of you is the one who looks ahead, designs a system, or hires assistants for the creative worker. Many of us have an unawakened manager and a very tired creative worker.

In my case, I was hiding from being a manager of my creative dream because I felt ill-equipped or incompetent to be a manager. Most managers I knew seemed like bossy tyrants, and I didn't want to be like that! Meanwhile, my creative worker was exhausted from overwork, because work is the only thing the creative worker knows how to do.

So I studied how to be a manager, and how that manager could provide assistance and care for my creative worker. I learned that I was a good and capable manager, and my creative dreams grew in new directions because of it. If you study and learn to activate your inner manager, you can design a system that truly supports growth. Otherwise, your creative worker will always be scrambling to "keep up."

My Dream Growth

ONE OF MY CREATIVE DREAMS was to have a company that would support my creative work and vision. I formed that company, Camp SARK, in 1993, and it produced over 200 products to support creative living, a magazine, and gave away "creative tool kits" for teachers. I also wrote and created 10 books during that time.

As my creative dreams grew, the structure of my company also grew. Growth involves change, focus, and strategy. I worked with a team of dedicated people and we all learned a lot about growing and about changing. I restructured Camp SARK in 2000, partly because it felt like it had grown too large.

"If you are distressed by anything external, the pain is not due to the thing itself, but to your estimate of it, and this you have the power to revoke at any moment."

Marcus Aurelius Antoninus

227

I discovered that growth isn't necessarily good if the system that supports that growth is faulty or becomes strained. I also learned that growth in business doesn't always match human growth.

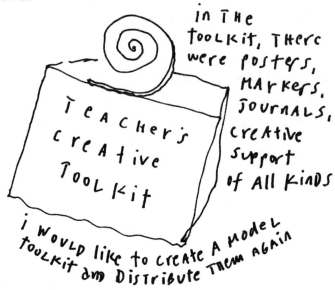

in THe tooLkit, THerc were posters, MArkers, journALs, creAtive support of All kinDs

TeACHer's creAtive TooL kit

i WouLD like to creAte A moDeL tooLkit anD Distribute THem AGAin

Teams

ANOTHER PART OF MANAGING and growing your creative dream is assembling a team to help you. Some of us have bad team memories: being chosen last, or not chosen at all. Joining a team and then not feeling a part of the team. Not knowing how to be part of a team.

Let's erase and rerecord any bad team memories.

Choose yourself first as your own team member and learn what you need to feel part of a team, and then give that to yourself.

We form teams all the time without calling it that. The dictionary says this team is: "A group of people working or playing together as a unit."

I think families are a kind of team. Growing creative dreams calls for us to form teams because we can create more in community than we can by ourselves.

You can create the type of team that works best for you.

A lot of creative dream-livers are isolated with their creative dreams and can greatly benefit from someone in addition to themselves working with their creative dreams.

When you make a creative dream real, it is then separate from you, and needs support in order to grow. A team is an excellent kind of support, and the right kind of team is the best type of support.

Marketing

GROWING YOUR CREATIVE DREAM may involve marketing. If you are at a public stage with your creative dream and wish to share it with more people, you will need to know something about marketing. It means literally "To bring to the marketplace."

When I began making my creative dreams available for people to purchase, I was plunged into the realm of marketing with little or no experience. I didn't study marketing, I just did it. I created art and words, people bought them, and that was my marketing training.

Actually, it works pretty well for a while, using a simple formula that most of us learned as children with lemonade stands: Whatever you offer for sale has to earn more than it costs you to make.

Since I had no formal business training, I didn't know about cost of sales or actual overhead, and many other valuable concepts about marketing. So as my creative dreams grew, my marketing expertise didn't grow at the same rate. I made enormous mistakes. For example, I sold T-shirts with my art printed on them, and took orders for large numbers of shirts. What I didn't fully calculate was the actual cost of the materials. As it turned out, I was actually losing money on every T-shirt I sold, which didn't become apparent until I'd been doing it for six months.

The stacks of posters grew taller than me

I also created 11,000 posters by hand in my garage, and forgot to calculate my actual time making them. As it turned out, my hourly rate was barely above minimum wage, once I figured in the supply costs.

I was still "successful" despite my marketing mistakes, and eventually hired a business mentor to teach me basic business and marketing so that I could grow my creative dreams even more skillfully.

If you choose to involve your creative dream in the world of trade and commerce, use some of your energy to become informed about what that means. It can be extremely exciting and rewarding to share your creative dream with the world and receive compensation in the form of money. You can then use that money to fund more creative dreams.

AT THE BEGINNING, you might make the simplest system, based on knowing how much your creative dream costs to make. These costs include:

Materials and supplies

Location

Your time

Later on, you can introduce the subjects of paying yourself first and reducing your location costs.

There are many free and low-cost resources for business education and marketing training, and this can be part of your creative dream growth. You can also use your team to assist you with marketing.

Scary or Alone Parts of "Success"

We can study and plan for success Differently

AS YOUR CREATIVE DREAM GROWS, you may encounter success. This success could greatly affect your creative dream, depending on how you handle it. Our society is a "success blesser," and success is intrinsically thought of as "good."

There isn't much information about the scary parts of success.

Success can:

Isolate or remove you from friends or familiar things

Distort your values

Overwhelm you

Cause you to quit your creative dream

The dictionary defines success as: "The gaining of position, fame, wealth, achievement, satisfaction." What's your definition?

How would you describe success in relationship to your creative dream?

Let's say your creative dream is to write a best-selling book. Have you considered these parts of success?

Friends and/or colleagues jealous and/or envious of you

More travel than you'd like

Fear of the next book and how will you match previous success

Best-seller lists and being on or off those lists

Public speaking

What if your success causes you to stop doing other things you enjoy?

Success is not the answer or a solution, but part of a greater system. Your response to and management of your success is pivotal in nourishing yourself and your creative dreams.

Success can:

Expand and accelerate your creative dream

Cause you to choose to be part of a team

Bring you in contact with wonderful people and things

Assist you in making your other creative dreams real

Support other people's creative dreams

Activate brand-new creative dreams

Success can also activate arrogance, egotism, and entitlement. It is good to have some supervision in the form of therapy or self-help literature to guide you in a positive direction.

Isolation with regard to creative dream-making can be an ongoing challenge. I recommend being part of a team—even if it's just one other person. Isolation is a choice, whether conscious or not, and does not promote growth. We can grow in solitude, but not as well in isolation. Discover the difference between the two and apply the results to your creative dreams.

Isolation promotes the belief that we are separate and alone. Solitude promotes the belief and space to learn to give to ourselves first, what we seek from others. This involves redefining solitude.

WHAT DOES IT MEAN to be overidentified with progress and/or success with regard to our creative dreams?

When we measure and determine who we are by what we do, we have forgotten what it means to be a succulent human bean.

We Are Succulent Human Beans

Our worthiness as humans comes from our existence first. Our actions can reinforce or act against that, but the truth of our worthiness is in our very being. Creative dreams made real can gain momentum quickly and cause us to think that we have value, or more value because of those dreams. Realize that your creative dream is not you, and gain objectivity about it. This will also serve you well as it grows and becomes even more separate from you. Your objectivity will allow you to gather feedback and suggestions for your creative dream without reacting with too much sensitivity.

Not taking anything about your creative dream personally

Calmly gathering facts about your creative dream

Studying the subject of objectivity

Your Creative Dream Growing Larger Than You

In the egg, hatched, infancy, and toddler stages, creative dreams are generally not larger than we are. We control their growth and their position. As dreams grow into child, adolescent, and adult stages, they can become larger than us.

This means that your creative dream is reaching and affecting more people than you can ever know. This creates a lot of energy, and can be managed in ways that bring you increased energy instead of draining you of energy.

If your creative dream has grown larger

than you, here are some things to know:

Energy can be studied and managed.

Misuse of energy can lead to feeling overwhelmed.

Supervised growth can help support a longer life for your creative dream.

Larger is not necessarily better—especially if there are insufficient systems to support it.

For example, if your creative dream leads people to contact you and you have no system for responding to them, this is energy lost.

Creative dream growth requires creative dream management. This management can be by you or

by someone else. I strongly advise learning to be your own manager before having someone else assist you in this way. Otherwise, you will not understand the purpose and results of management. You might also work with inferior management just to get things done. You will need to untangle these things later.

Many creative dream-livers do not foresee the growth of their creative dreams. They imagine it either never happening or being a tremendous success, with nothing in the middle.

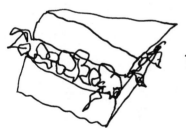

its Like A sandwich:
There's a lot of good stuff
in The middle

The middle is where you build your support and foundations for long-term growth. The middle is

where you can make more mistakes with fewer consequences. You can manage and guide your creative dream growth with knowledge, power, and intuition.

Your creative dreams made real need:

Your focused attention in an objective way

Creation of new types of support for growth

Places to go for help when things aren't working

Business and financial planning in advance

A system that works for your creative dream when you're not there

All of the above requires you to have or be a manager.

We are not just born as managers. Some people have greater aptitude for it. I believe that anyone can learn management skills.

Begin to notice when you are acting as a manager for your creative dreams. This may feel unfamiliar or uncomfortable at first. The creative worker part of you is used to making reactive, emotion-based decisions dependent on mood and energy. The manager part of you makes objective fact-based decisions from a rational place, independent of mood and energy.

You can support your inner manager by attending conferences or classes in this subject, and discussing your experiences with other creative workers evolving their inner managers.

Remember: creative workers often try to do it all by themselves; managers always look for assistance.

If you form or join a team, this action is coming from your inner manager and will involve your learning what that inner manager needs.

Growing your creative dreams will lead you into new parts of yourself and your life. I invite you to create new support systems for that growth.

You Can Explore Growth in the Following Ways

1. Assess Your Management Skills and Aptitude

See if you can determine whether you are primarily a creative worker with regard to your creative dream, or whether you are also managing your creative dream. When you determine how active your manager is, you will know how to proceed to obtain increased assistance.

2. Accelerate Your Creative Dream

Do this by:

Visualizing (imagine what it could be like)

Intending (writing down and making your intentions real)

Asking (have someone witness your growth process)

Doing (take one action toward growth)

3. Make an Assistant's List

If you had an assistant, what would that person do? Add to this list every time you think of something you don't personally need to be doing.

4. Locate Resources for Your Business Education

Search online

Visit the library

Ask your team

Assemble information about marketing and managing

My Assistant would:
1. Pay the bills
2. Answer emails
3. Organize things
4.
5.
6.

Keep adding to this list

One of the most important areas to explore about growth is how you **actually like** to live and work.

If you like working alone at your own pace, you could be very unhappy with growth that asks you to work with others at an uncomfortable pace. If you like working with others, they need to have similar goals and values, or your growth could be compromised.

How do you imagine your creative dream growth best serving you?

You can write a detailed list and description of what kind of growth will work best for you. Being detailed and thorough is important. One time I made a list about the type of person I wanted to move into my apartment building. The list included details like: "Makes homemade soup" and "Plays the piano." What I forgot to ask for was someone who could socially relate. For all the years this person lived near me, we rarely spoke at all!

GROWTH is not only something that happens. It is something you can choose and have influence over.

Your creative dreams will benefit from those choices.

I support you in choosing conscious, healthy, grounded growing experiences.

As my creative dreams have grown and changed, I've learned a great deal about growth and how it affects me. I've experienced unconscious, unhealthy, and ungrounded growth, and the opposite. Both types of growth have been great teachers, and I now choose the healthier variety more often.

Consider growth carefully, tend to it well, and this growth will serve you and your creative dreams.

Energizing Eleventh Month

Managing and Growing Your Creative Dreams

☆

week one

A Game or Something to Try

Invent Your Dream Work Environment

As you and your creative dreams grow and change, you might wish to change your work environment. You can do this in your imagination first, and discover what really delights you.

239

Here are some questions to start with:

What does it look like?

Describe all the details: furniture, equipment, wall, window and floor coverings, paint colors, shape, and size

Where is it located?

Create a detailed description

When do you work there?

What is your dream schedule?

Are other people in this space?

If so, describe them and what they specifically do

How do you feel working here?

List the qualities

week two

A G I F T for You

I SEND YOU . . .

An imaginary team to support your creative dream life. This team is "paid" by your trust fund (your trust fund is a redefinition of the usual trust fund, and is based on the amount of trust you have in yourself and in life).

Your team consists of:

CHEF AND PERSONAL NUTRITIONIST: Delicious, perfectly nutritious meals appear whenever you want them.

VIRTUAL ASSISTANT: This person works from his or her own office, and assists you in every administrative way.

MARKETING CONSULTANT: Advises you about bringing your creations to the world.

FINANCIAL WIZARDRY: A team of consultants who oversee your money and continually expand your resources.

PERSONAL AND BUSINESS COACH: Person or persons who consult with you in every area of your life to help you make your creative dreams real.

VACATION PLANNER: Juicy, succulent places to go, with options and choices for you to consider.

HEALTH-CARE COORDINATOR: Makes health-care appointments, follows up with you, keeps records, inspires you to be even healthier.

ELDER-CARE CONSULTANT: For your healthiest aging, and for those you love, oversees every aspect of care.

SPIRITUAL ADVISER: For the care of your soul and spiritual direction.

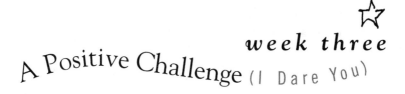

week three

A Positive Challenge (I Dare You)

Describe and define the kind of team that would most benefit you and your creative dream. This can be an actual or imaginary team.

How many members?

What kinds of people?

Where and when does it meet?

How are the meetings set up?

What services does your team provide?

How do you feel being part of this team?

If you're already part of a team, assess its effectiveness and current place in your life.

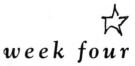

RADIANT Resources *week four*

Orbiting the Giant Hairball: A Corporate Fool's Guide to Surviving with Grace
Gordon MacKenzie

Self-Promotion for the Creative Person: Get the Word Out About What You Are and What You Do
Les Silber

Prosperity Pie: How to Relax About Money and Everything Else
SARK

Sell Yourself without Selling Your Soul: A Woman's Guide to Promoting Herself, Her Business, Her Product or Her Cause with Integrity and Spirit
Susan Harrow

The E-Myth Revisited: Why Most Small Businesses Fail and What to Do About It
Michael Gerber

Turning the Mind into an Ally
Sakyong Mipham

The Power of Now
Eckhart Tolle

Dream Big
Lisa Hammond

www.promoteyourcreativity.com
www.assistu.com
www.susanharrow.com
www.creativelee.com
www.pobronson.com
www.mcnairwilson.com

Dream Stoppers (Old Thoughts)

Honoring These Thoughts

1. I've wasted too much time, it's too late now.

2. Other people are living my dreams.

3. My dreams will never work.

4. I've tried for too long and I'm a failure.

5. I can't seem to start.

6. What if I choose the wrong dream? It's easier not to try.

7. It's just too much work.

8. My real life takes all my time and energy.

9. My family needs me to be practical.

10. After all, how many people get to live their dreams?

Dream Starters
(New Thoughts)

Welcoming These Thoughts

1. Nothing is lost or wasted. There is plenty of time for my dreams and every moment counts.

2. My dreams are as individual as I am. No one can live them but me.

3. My dreams work easily.

4. I'm choosing new attitudes and perspectives and intend to live my dreams actively.

5. I begin easily and develop habits of completion.

6. All my dreams are interesting and I now find it easy to explore them.

7. My dream living work is easy and fun.

8. My dream life and real life are the same life. I now have even more energy for both.

9. My family supports and loves my dream life.

10. I am one of many, many people joyfully living my dreams.

Questions and
Answers

about Creative Dream Living
☆

IN THE 15 YEARS I've been actively teaching and talking about creative dreams, I've been fascinated by the questions that are asked. Each person asking a question assists many more people than she can know. I love these questions. Here are some of the most often asked, along with my answers and thoughts.

Q: How can microMOVEments really work? The movements are so small and I don't have that much time left!

A: Is what you're currently doing working faster? Have you actually tried microMOVEments in regard to your creative dream? Or are you in your head about it?

Q: What if I simply don't have time to live my dream?

A: You don't actually have the time. You create the time. You paste seconds and moments together and they become hours, days, weeks, months, and years. You choose to commit your time to what makes your heart leap.

Q: What if my dream isn't going to make me any money?

A: Money is not and cannot be the only measurement of success of creative dreams. Review your choices and commitments and see if you need to do something else to make money and support your creative dreams.

Q: It seems like my belief systems consistently undermine my dreams. What can I do?

A: Study, review, practice, and revise your belief systems. Choose to have your belief systems be in alignment with your creative dreams.

Q: I feel like I have too many dreams and am overwhelmed about where to start.

A: Feeling overwhelmed is often a defense against choosing. See if you can unravel the feeling and see what's really there. You cannot have "too many dreams." See your numbers of dreams as abundance.

Q: How long do I stay with, struggle for, or try my dream?

A: Does it feel "juicy?" Does it give you something most days? If not, it may be time to release or retire that particular dream. You have not lost or wasted any time.

Q: When does quitting a creative dream make sense?

A: When it hurts or depletes you. When you're consistently stuck, blocked, or negative about it. When it isn't nourishing.

Q: I have no idea what my dream is. What should I do?

A: Visit with your "inside children" and ask them. If that doesn't work, explore your inner critics with the help of books and/or tapes.

Q: I thought I was living my dream, but it feels flat or stale, or like too much work.

A: Sometimes it's us that are flat and stale. The creative dream is often just waiting for us to reenergize. If it consistently feels like too much work, consider approaching your dream differently.

Q: I feel scared to really live my dream. How do I take that leap?

A: Instead of leaping you can crawl. We don't need to only make dramatic changes in order to live our dreams.

Q: I think my job is causing me to forget my dreams.

A: This is very common and can temporarily feel true. We sometimes blame our jobs and try to change them instead of doing interior work and changing ourselves.

Q: My creative dream keeps changing and I don't know what to do.

A: Congratulate yourself on having an active fast-moving dream! Then study how to manage your creative dream.

Q: I thought my dream would make money by now and it isn't. Do I keep trying or do something else?

A: If your frustration is fueling you, keep trying. If it's draining you, try something else.

Q: I'm pretty far along with my creative dream, but I need help! Any suggestions?

A: Be specific about the type of help you need.

Q: I think I've outgrown my dream. How can I tell?

A: You might have grown it as far as it can go. Review the stages of dreams on page 36.

Q: What if microMOVEments really haven't worked for me? What do you recommend?

A: Have you really worked for them? Give examples.

Q: How can I get more support for my creative dream? I feel lonely a lot of the time.

A: Review support systems on page 105 and consider starting or joining a group or team.

Q: What if I'm not ready to start living my dream?

A: Nothing is lost or wasted. You may be gathering knowledge, energy, or resources. Recognize this as your choice and celebrate it.

Q: What if I'm doing my dream and it isn't working?

A: Describe and define what "isn't working." List what you've completed. Choose to describe your efforts differently.

Q: How do I know if my dream is my "real dream" or I am doing someone else's dream for me?

A: If you are fulfilled by the process of your dream, it is your real dream.

CHAPTER TWELVE

Twelfth Month Tender

Living Elegantly and Successfully with Your Creative Dreams

The purpose of this chapter is to support and encourage a healthy model of success and celebration with regard to your creative dreams.

Elegant, Successful You!

I CAN SEE YOU NOW, living elegantly and successfully with one or more of your creative dreams in full bloom. This does not mean you will not falter, flail, procrastinate, or practice perfectionism or avoidance. It means that you will have learned to do those things elegantly. Or you can practice. You will have learned to balance gracefully on the difference between what you envision and what actually happens.

Making creative dreams real involves a lot of loss, change, and destruction. We will lose our former construct. We will change our minds, our direction, and the descriptions of our creative dreams.

We can destroy what stops us, stifles us, or makes us believe that we cannot make our creative dreams real. This is a positive type of destruction.

We can stop staring down to find what's lost or broken—we can look straight ahead with a gleam in our eyes. Our creative dreams deserve our full and consistent attention. We are made with elegance and style, and can apply that to our creative dream-living.

Go ahead! Describe yourself as elegant.

The dictionary says elegance is "a tasteful luxuriousness of grace and style, design and content." Change this definition if you need to. Reshape the definition to fit who you are now, who you will become, and for all the times you feel clunky, ragged, or in turmoil. You can locate the elegance in those states too.

It is time to identify ourselves and our creative dreams in this luxurious fashion. We cannot wait until we "get there" or until dreams get done.

Declare yourself elegantly doing it now!

How Open Are You to Change?

CREATIVE DREAMS ARE chockablock with change. As soon as creative dreams start moving and becoming real, they and you have already changed.

This may be alarming if you didn't foresee change or practice your change-acceptance skills.

The best ways to prepare for change are:

1. Updating and expanding your self-care skills.

"in our life there is a single color, as on an artist's palette, which provides the meaning of life and art. It is the color of love"
MARC CHAGALL

These include:

Nutrition and exercise

> Are these systems working? Any changes or upgrades needed?

Support systems

> Who and what are yours? Any expansion needed?

Psychological systems

> How do you feel and how do you support your psychological growth and changes?

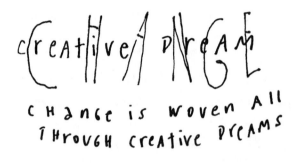

CHANGE is woven ALL
THROUGH CREATIVE DREAMS

2. Increasing your ability to work with energy.

This includes:

"Running energy" in your body.

Learn how energy moves in your body and how to manage it.

Grounding yourself

> Occupying both your mind and your body at the same time and being aware when you're not.

Assessing your energy

> Learning to evaluate and provide what you need energetically.

3. Joining or starting a team or a group

Do this for:

Validation

This will remind you that you're not the only one.

Acknowledgement

This will help you to "take in" what you're accomplishing.

Company or community

We gain strength being witnessed by community.

Strength or power

Owning our strength and power can be practiced in groups differently from what we can do by ourselves.

Explore your **possible resistance to change** and in what ways you might try to prevent change (even positive change). Change can be unsettling and scary, as well as exciting. The more you know about your responses to change, the more choices and options you will have.

Sharing Dreams with Others

YOUR DREAM MAY GROW to the size that makes you want to share it with others, or you may just wish to share it.

I believe that it is important to uncover your motivation for sharing. A big question to ask is:

"Am I afraid or nervous to pursue my creative dream alone?"

Please consider the possibility that your creative dream may need to be realized by just you. You can use teams, groups, or assistants, but the dream itself is yours. Sometimes people abdicate or try to dilute the power of their creative dream by sharing it with others unconsciously, prematurely, or based on fear. If you share your creative dream for the wrong reasons, it is unfair to you and to the people you share it with.

Examine your motives carefully and if you choose to share your creative dream, do it:

Wholeheartedly

With healthy boundaries

Consciously and carefully

Creative Dreams in Service

ONE OF THE BEST THINGS about making creative dreams real is your opportunity to have your dream be of service to others. Creative dreams love to be used for this purpose.

Whatever your creative dream is, ask how it can serve others, and then decide how and when you will provide service. Some creative dreams are inherently service based; others can be set up that way.

If you think of your creative dream as a service provider, people and places will materialize to make use of your offerings.

MOST OF US ARE INSPIRED TO "HELP OTHERS" and often don't take specific action to make that happen consistently. Creative dreams can be consistent service providers in the answers to the following questions:

Can and how will your creative dream be of service?

What can you set up now to create opportunities to serve?

Which kinds of things, as a result of your creative dreams, can be expanded upon and shared with others?

We don't need extensive programs in order to be of service. We can begin now, at whatever stage we're at with our creative dreams, and share our:

Time

Energy

Products

KNOWLEDGE

Connections

I believe that every company and creative dream needs to be set up with this in mind. We could expand "service stations" to include refueling for people in all kinds of situations.

Welcome New Creative Dreams

Why aren't we adopting schools the way we adopt highways to keep them clean? One of my creative dreams is to set up an easy system for people and communities to adopt schools and funnel money and supplies to that particular school. This would be online, nationwide, and enormously successful.

Our capacity for service is enormous and our creative dreams are leaping to be employed in this way. YOU are the channel and vehicle for those creative dreams and the services they can provide.

Welcoming New Creative Dreams

AGE AND TIME have very little to do with creative dreams. We can continue creating and dreaming new dreams all of our lives.

As dreams become real, creative new dreams will begin appearing. At first, these new creative dreams will be at the egg stage and may never develop from there.

A number of new creative dreams may tumble in during a nap, and you might hatch them right away. When you become even more experienced at making creative dreams real, creative dream development can be an even faster process.

The act of making creative dreams real causes more dreams to develop. You will continue to attract new ideas and people in the creative dream realms, and the more you hatch new dreams, the more will float into view.

Create a welcoming atmosphere by:

Releasing your creative dreams after you have made them real.

Not hoarding creative dream ideas as though you won't get new ones.

Planning to receive new creative dreams all through your life.

Living your life as a creative dream.

Welcome your creative dreams into your life, and let us see and experience them. The world is a receptive magnet for everyone's creative dreams.

We are abundantly endowed with

Rich

imaginations and endless

creativity

I invite us all to creatively dream

eVen BIGGeR

than we ever have.

Celebrating and
Acknowledging

WHAT CAN YOU CELEBRATE about your creative dream?

Sometimes we wait to celebrate until "things are done" and forget how or why to celebrate along the way.

Every tiny movement in the direction of your creative dreams deserves celebration.

Celebrations can be:

Exterior:

Sharing with friends about your Creative Dream movements

Doing an activity in honor of your creative dreams

Sending out e-mail descriptions and updates

Reporting to your Creative Dream Team

Interior:

Writing in your creative dream guidebook or journal

Napping, resting, eating nourishing food

Joy-full physical activity

We can Do More celebrating Along The Way

If you haven't made any movements in the direction of your creative dreams, this also deserves celebration. We deserve to celebrate ourselves all along the way, not only when we are "accomplishing" or "producing."

The process of living our creative dreams is as important as the progress. Invent celebrations for your micromovements, inventions, brand-new ideas, and solutions. Keep your eye out for moments to celebrate. We often become overly focused on outcomes and conclusions.

Celebrate your mistakes! Every mistake is a teacher and can lead to new successes. I have made so many mistakes in business that led me into a situation I would never have been aware of if not for the "mistake." Celebrate quitting, delaying, or not deciding. Again, these are all teachers. Everything I've quit, delayed, or not decided has exposed me to learn new ways of doing things.

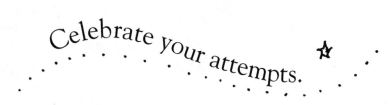

Celebrate your attempts.

Whatever you've tried has benefited you in some way. Illuminate that benefit and choose to celebrate it.

My friend Craig McNair Wilson uses a saying in his life and business that I admire:

Assume Brilliance

He is also creating a new book that will be called "YES, AND . . .": *Brainstorming Secrets of a Theme Park Designer*. Visit www.mcnairwilson.com.

One of the most beautiful things about creative dreams is how much there is to celebrate and acknowledge.

MY FRIEND JENNIFER quit her corporate job and moved to Italy to teach English. While living in a tiny medieval village, she fell in love with an Italian Buddhist man named Paolo. They are being married this fall in Italy and asked me to perform the ceremony! Here is some of what she had to say about her creative dreams:

Jennifer

What have you done to live your creative dreams?

I moved to a tiny city in Italy, without the language, the encouragement of a friend, or the security of my family nearby. I had given up unfulfilling work, big paychecks, and an exciting lifestyle. I gave myself the precious commodity of time. I looked inside and started to live from what I found, my essence. I wasn't on a mission to find love, but to open my life and live in a more meaningful way. I cut the cord of security, safety, and comfortable sameness and that "dangerous move" has yielded what I hoped would come to me in the safety.

What are you willing to do?

I am willing to risk future pain, regret, and heartache, which are all possible when you agree to love someone. He may become sick, he may deceive me, he may disappoint me. I am willing to believe he won't, and continue on. My marriage will change the relationships I have with my incredible parents and sister, and all my wonderful friends. I am willing to accept those changes and do the work necessary to interweave this new relationship into those that have supported me up to this point. I guess I am willing to fail, and therefore feel fearless.

What advice would you give to anyone wanting to live his or her creative dreams?

If you have creative dreams, you are already living them in part. Not all parts of the world breed creativity and dreaming and the idea that you can really do anything you want to do. Living your dreams in your dreams is a beautiful and safe arena, but to risk and bring one or two of those dreams into the real world, that is really living. Don't wait until you have all the answers, because you never will. Listen to yourself. You know exactly what you want to do with your life. Sometimes a giant step, something really drastic, is easier than millions of tiny steps in the direction of your dreams. Huge, unproductive pauses in the action are necessary for the magical workings of dreams. Surround yourself with believers in you and write down what you want.

I would like to acknowledge Jennifer for her courage and willingness.

MY FRIEND BILL was recently cast in the Broadway production of *Little Shop of Horrors*.

He says,

I have been reunited with my PASSION after "losing" it for many years. I had lost faith in myself and lost sight of my dreams. I feel TALENTED, energetic, competent,

YOUNG, sexy, WORTHWHILE. AND because I believe it (and behave as if I believe it) others believe it too.

Creative dreams keep life in balance. Without them life would be a black-and-white silent film day in, day out. With creative dreams we get to be part of a Technicolor Ziegfeld extravaganza.

I wanted to celebrate and acknowledge Bill's feelings of success. It is often scarier to describe our successes than our failures, and we can choose to change this.

MY FRIEND ILENE reveals what stops her about her creative dream, and I want to celebrate her realizations:

Nothing scares me about it. What has stopped me from living this FULLY has been my own process. The process of ownership of my Self. I have always owned my talent, my skill, my devotion to people. What I have not owned, until quite recently, is the love of myself. It is consistently SHOCKING to me how resistant I have been in regard to this!! I have been told 5,000 times that I am special, wonderful, etc., but until I felt it myself, these were only beautiful words that engendered good feelings for a few minutes. I find this both sad and glorious. Sad that it has taken so long and glorious that it has come in the time of elder influence. I am 72 and healthy. I am planning on the next 25 years of life to be the happiest and most cosmically productive years of my life . . .

I acknowledge Ilene's journey toward even more self-love.

MY FRIEND JOE shares one of his newer creative dreams and speaks about a "creative dream drought."

Joe Brown

Do you have a creative dream or dreams?

To create a newspaper section that helps bring the widest range of people to the arts and creative use of their time, and to encourage the creative people and garden the arts, helping them to grow in my unbelievably rich area.

Would you describe yourself as living your creative dream?

Now, after a long period of creative drought, long dark YEARS of the soul, I've found my way to my creative dream, and it has found its way to me! One phrase that stayed with me during the dry, dark period when I wondered if I would ever find my way back to my creative self is a Quaker saying: "Proceed as way opens." Think about that.

What inspires or excites you with regard to creative dreams?

I feel plugged in now. Literally. Like I'm electric, all of a sudden, and time doesn't matter, the hours and days and weeks are too short, and I'm full of ideas and I'm hearing other people's ideas, and things seems possible. And it's not manic or out of control. I can let it drop and enjoy life when I'm not working. That's how I know it's in balance.

What advice would you give to anyone wanting to live his or her creative dreams?

Be patient. As I noted before, proceed as way opens. Endure the dry periods. Know that it's all adding up to something. I worked in catering, floral design, event planning, freelance writing, and public relations before signing back on with the newspaper. I used to ask God, "Why this?" when I would find myself in a strange new job, wondering what it could possibly be adding up to. Well, it did all add up. Everything I learned during those wildly disparate jobs, I've ended up using. And there are things I learned that I know I'll use someday! Most of all, while I was working in jobs that my friends and family considered strange or not suited to me, I was learning what work was really all about. I don't take it for granted anymore. I know how lucky I am.

And I know that I have certain talents and gifts.

I would like to honor Joe for his patience and faith, and say congratulations!

I would like to acknowledge and celebrate Andrea, Katie, Mike, and Patricia. Each one is a dear soul and a friend. Here are excerpts of their responses to my questions:

Andrea Scher, ARTIST

www.superherodesigns.com

Do you have a creative dream or dreams?

Yes, daily! Coming up with dreams is never the problem, it's choosing which dreams I'd like to go after (and when) that poses a challenge. I'm your buffet-of-dreams kind of girl. I like to taste a bit of everything.

Would you describe yourself as living your creative dream or dreams? Why or why not?

I am living many of my dreams. It's funny. Once you start living your dreams, you forget that they were ever these seemingly unattainable things. They just become your life, and every once in a while you get a glimpse of how remarkable that is, that you ARE in fact living something extraordinary. You created something that wasn't there before.

I had a dream of making a living from my art, and I'm doing it! This seems like a miracle to me. Now this original dream is growing new appendages. I want to write books, be a photographer, paint more . . . I love that there is never an end to the dreams we have; one just inspires the next.

I just married my true love, Matt, recently, a huge creative dream that I am just beginning to live. Motherhood will be the next and biggest dream of all. I feel like I've only scratched the surface.

Katie Grant Alden

Do you have a creative dream or dreams?

To be an awe-inspiring actress, an interior designer, an author, a playwright, a producer and director of film and stage, and to create an alternative healing center.

What do you think would help you live more of your creative dreams?

What would and does help is doing little things each day that bring me closer to my dream like meditation, prayer, study, practice, research, exercise, taking care of myself, affirmations, meeting and talking with those that are living the same dream, and mainly admitting that I have these dreams, that I deserve them, and that I can make them happen.

Mike, PERSONAL AND BUSINESS COACH

www.mike-robbins.com

Would you describe yourself as living your creative dream or dreams? Why or why not?

I am definitely living my creative dream as it regards my book. My book proposal is done and I have it in front of some potential publishers right now. I am excited, but also scared about rejection.

Do you think that the living of one dream stops you or slows you down from living others? If so, please explain.

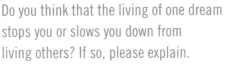

I think that I often get so focused on one thing, it is hard for me to focus on something else . . . especially when it is big. Working on my book over the past year and half has taken a lot of mental, emotional, spiritual, and physical energy. At times, it has taken me away from really being present and loving with the people in my life and it definitely has taken me away from pursuing other dreams. However, going after one's dream can be so inspiring and empowering, it makes us see the infinite possibilities in life and in our other dreams as well.

How or why are your creative dreams important to you?

Because creativity is the juice of life. Being creative is the most brilliant and powerful expression of my feminine energy and I feel alive being creative. It is also very challenging and rewarding for me to be creative.

Patricia, LIFE COACH

www.patriciahuntington.com

My creative dream is what I have established in my life today. It is that I live beautifully and quietly and do my life's work creatively. Occasionally there is a downturn in the economy and that scares me until I realize that in truth I am just the emanation of my creator and will always be safe and cared for. I am inspired by the work that I do and the work that I dream of doing and the dream of life I live inside myself. That creative dream life is filled with wonder and affluence and beauty and art and splendid relationships with people whom I adore.

Description of my dream yet to be lived . . . I am in a wondrous building that is really a home with an office suite attached to it. There are Persian carpets and works of art in this magic space that suits me totally. The windows overlook the ocean and appear to be moving paintings, always changing. There is nature everywhere around this place and there is a big kitchen where the resident chef cooks amazing healthy food for me and my guests. There are great flower arrangements everywhere and the furniture is elegant and comfortable. I am surrounded with music from a built-in stereo system and there is a plasma TV built into the area about the fireplace. It appears to be a painting and as I push a button the painting moves and the screen is there behind it. The energy in this place is warm and inviting and useful. I dream of the feeling I have being in this place, a feeling of belonging and fitting into my surroundings. I dream of this feeling more that I dream of any one thing in particular. I dream of talking to people and uplifting spirits.

I would encourage people to learn how to dream creatively. I would tell them to find a book that explains what a creative dream is and follow the path to that dream . . . My creative dreams are important to me because they are what I am. I think that creative dreams are from God and that they have everything to do with our purpose in life. Thank you and good night . . . Patricia the dreamer.

Share Your Success with the World

AS YOUR CREATIVE DREAMS grow and develop, we want to hear about your success. This success can include the parts that haven't worked so well. There's a great quote:

> *"Success is going from failure to failure with no loss of enthusiasm."*—WINSTON CHURCHILL

Your enthusiasm for success is a magnet for more success.

What does success mean to you?

One of my definitions is: "To be creatively of use to myself and the world."

When we hear or read of others' successes, we can use them as role models. We can adopt new methods and systems for our creative dreams. If we get envious or jealous of others' successes, we can look at what we might like to develop for ourselves.

Some of my creative dreams that weren't successful actually led me to success in other areas.

269

I had a creative dream of riding a camel across Africa. As I gathered information about camels, Africa, and being a woman alone on a camel in Africa, I decided not to follow through on that particular dream. I wrote my first book instead.

Sometimes success **means** choosing differently. I have successfully chosen differently many times!

Success is not measured only by conventional standards. When I succeeded in keeping journals about my life, people judged their success by the fact that they were unpublished. I went on to publish much of the material in those journals.

I recommend delving into your beliefs about success and your relationship to success. Your ability to change and redefine success and what it means to you will have a great effect on your creative dreams.

We are all inspired by success and by people successfully living their creative dreams. We are also inspired by all the detours, wrong turns, and things that don't work.

When I started writing my books and sharing my faults and flaws, I wondered how people would respond and react. The more I shared what I actually felt or experienced, the more people supported me. I felt really surprised by this. I had believed that "success shows no weakness," and that to succeed meant never failing, or if you did fail, cover it up immediately.

I am glad to see and experience our world changing to accommodate new definitions of success, and to stop sheltering cover-ups. Every system we have is undergoing these changes, and this is a good thing.

It also means that creative dream-livers are needed more than ever. Each floundering system is in need of creative alternatives and solutions. We can all participate by making our creative dreams real, and then considering making those dreams available to be of service to others.

Our creative dream power is enormous.

Let's share even more of ourselves and our creative dreams.

I will be learning and practicing all of the things in this book.

You are heartily invited to join me!

C r e a t i v e l y   d r e a m i n g ,

Susan Ariel Rainbow Kennedy

aka SARK

San Francisco, California
September 8, 2003

Tender Twelfth Month
Living Elegantly and Successfully with Your Creative Dreams

week one

A Game or Something to Try

Celebrate and Acknowledge Yourself
in Positive Ways

Take a day or part of a day and decide to speak about celebrating yourself. Think about what there is to celebrate and acknowledge and make a point to speak of it. These things can be any size. Keep the focus on yourself.

You could say to a friend,

"I'm celebrating my willingness to go to the gym."

"I'm celebrating the new plants in my garden."

"I'm acknowledging my ability to be present in difficult conversations."

"I'm acknowledging my capacity for tenderness."

blanket yourself with acknowledgement

Notice how it feels to do this. See what arises as you spend a day in this way.

A GIFT for You   *week two*

I SEND YOU . . .

The awareness that you are inspiring. You are inspiring to me, reading this book. You are inspiring to me in the following ways: For your tiny and large kindnesses, for your glad heart and your confused tears, for your stumbling and yearning. For your endearing

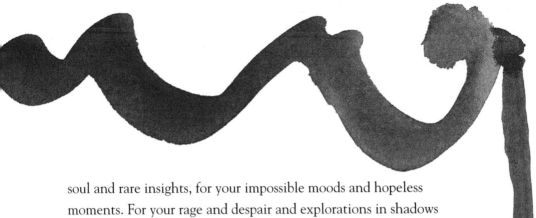

soul and rare insights, for your impossible moods and hopeless moments. For your rage and despair and explorations in shadows and darkness, for your resistance and conflict and refusal to feel good, or do good things. For your selflessness and especially for your selfishness. For your pathetic vulnerable times and for all your splendidly human moments. For your incandescent spirit and ingenious escapes. For your will and suffering. For everything that you've tried to hide. For your failings and attempts and for all that you have lost and found. For your regrets and loneliness and for every fear that has ever stalked you. For your neurotic bumbling. For radiant knowledge and countless expressions of love. You are inspiring to me because you are exquisitely YOU.

week three

A Positive Challenge (I Dare You)

Call for Good Things

I recommend the following phone messages for good energy:

☆ 415/546-3742 (EPIC)

SARK's 24-hour "Inspiration Line: A place to be how you actually are." This line just celebrated its 10th anniversary, and

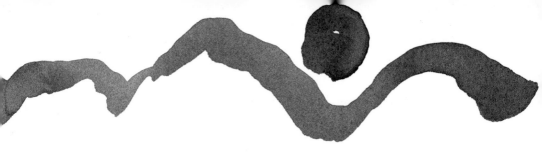

people call from all over the world. I listen to most of the messages and record a new message when the spirit moves me.

900/950-7700

Rob Brezsny's free-will astrology line. Although it costs money (about $6 per call) it's packed full of illuminated gems and the message changes weekly.

week four

R A D I A N T Resources

The Joy Diet: 10 Daily Practices for a Happier Life
   Martha Beck

Take Time for Your Life: A Personal Coach's Seven-Step Program for Creating the Life You Want
   Cheryl Richardson

How Much Joy Can You Stand? A Creative Guide to Facing Your Fears and Making Your Dreams Come True
   Suzanne Falter-Barnes

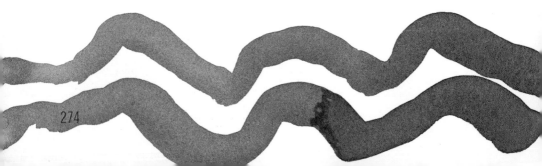

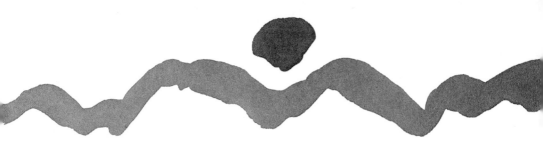

*The Right Questions: Ten Essential Questions
to Guide You to an Extraordinary Life*
   Debbie Ford

*Letting Go of the Person You Used to Be: Lessons on Loss, Change,
and Spiritual Transformation*
   Lama Surya Das

Journal of a Solitude
   May Sarton

www.innerlinks.com
www.soundstrue.com

415/546-3742: SARK's Inspiration Line

Juicy Living Cards, by SARK.
A 50-card full color deck,
double-sided!
These are luminous cards of
encouragement and inspiration.
Available from
www.hayhouse.com or
www.planetsark.com

This is an example of a Juicy Living Card!

acknowledgments

I deeply acknowledge and celebrate the many souls who inspire and support my creative dreams.

TO MY READERS, who inspire me to fill myself with creative energy and fresh enthusiasm . . .

TO MY MOTHER, "Marvelous Marjorie," who died on October 8, 2003, after 80 glorious years (and she would add, some *not* so glorious!)

TO MY DEAR FRIEND, Isabel, who died on September 11, 2003, after 90 splendid years.

I see them both as having graduated to greater realms.

To my vibrant tribe of truth-telling friends and family: I love and squeeze each of you!

Andrew Andrea, Matt Bill, May-Ree, Chellie, Steve, Sidney, Kim Bibbo, Judy, Silvana **Bill Hubner** Brigette, Martine Craig McNair Wilson **Claire North** Cheri Huber Debra, Steven, Emma, Bodhi **Debbie Edwards** Elissa, Alex, Charlie Emily Claire, Cheryl, Mark Eleanor Traubman Ilene Cummings Jupiter Jen, Paolo Joshua Kadison Jason, Erika Jan, Marina Joe Brown Jude, John Karen, John Kathryn, Aja Katie Grant Larry Rosenthal Lois, John Linda, Bryce Luchina, David, Giles Leigh, Jason, Avery Maggie Oman Shannon Merrell Mike Robbins Mary Ann, Tim, Josephine Nikki Neighbors: Sally, Jimmie, Marti, Lea, John, Michael Patricia Huntington, Brandy Ray Davi Robin, John Robyn Posin Roy Carlisle Sabrina Suzanne, Denoon Tanya, Ben Sam, Steve Tori Nethery Vanessa Carlisle Virginia Bell Val, Clark, Jonah Yofe, David Zoe, Oliver, Adrienne, Ken

AFTER ALPHABETIZING THIS LIST, I would like to note that I have openings for friends whose first names begin with the letters F, G, H, N, O, Q, U, W, X

A SPECIAL NOTE OF THANKS to my Mom's caregivers: Senior Abilities Unlimited, Peterson Home Care and Pathfinder. Also to Kathy Green!

Deep gratitude to: Cathy & Marc, Dick & Marilyn, Kathleen & Chris, Patty Lee, Bob Blackmur, and all the dear friends and relatives who loved and cared for my mother. Bless Phyllis Mackenzie for her sister love.

I deeply thank and acknowledge my deluxe team of professionals who assist me in growing Camp SARK, and in living my creative work dreams.

Their energy, focus, enthusiasm and dedication are greatly appreciated: Anne Ferguson, Tammi Riedl, Andrea Scher, Jillian Banks, Larry Rosenthal, Irving Bernstein, Marc Coffey, Leslie Bruhn, Patricia Huntington, David Culot, Nate Stone, Patrick Vilain.

Special thanks to Andrea Scher and Craig McNair Wilson for book design consultation.

I am very grate*full to my health care professionals: Dr. Kristine Hicks, Dr. Sam Rhame, Dr. Gary Ross, Patricia Huntington, Regan, Leo and his creative dental team, Dr. Jenny Taylor (Jupiter's doctor), Scott Kaminski.

Thanks to my marketing partners: Amber Lotus, Hay House, Femail Creations, Celestial Arts, Simon & Schuster.

Enduring thanks to my literary agents, the Creative Culture: their commitment and support are visible in the pages of this book and in my writing life. Thank you, Debra Goldstein, Mary Ann Naples, Nicole Diamond Austin.

Thank you! to my publisher Simon & Schuster and the team of people that help make such great books: Trish Todd, Brett Valley, Cherlynne Li, Joy O'Meara, Jim Thiel, and the whole team at Fireside.

Special thanks to Jill Weber for such creative design work.

Accolades to Faren Bachelis for unusual copyediting.

Thanks to my first publisher, Celestial Arts, who helped make my creative dreams of being a published author REAL.

come over to my web-sight to play and be supported with your creative dreams

resources

MY COMPANY IS CALLED **Camp SARK** and we create products and services to **inspire** and **support** creative dream-living.

Come see me at:

www.planetsark.com

THERE ARE SO MANY **wonder-full** things to do at Planet SARK, including:

Being part of the **free** "Marvelous Message Board" creative community

Visiting the "Magic Cottage Store" for books and other products

Receiving a **free** e-letter from me (*e* stands for energy)

Reading or posting a message in my "Glorious Guest Book"

Call my inspiration line: 415-546-EPIC (3742) for a free 5-minute recording by me. This is a serendipitous place to "be how you actually are."

Call my information line: 415-397-SARK (7275) for latest news, products, and upcoming events.

All kindred spirits welcome